The Artist's Way

Julia Cameron is an active artist who teaches internationally.
A poet, playwright, fiction writer and essayist, she has extensive credits
in film, television and theatre, and is an award-winning journalist.
She is the author of the bestselling books on creative practice
The Artist's Way and *The Vein of Gold*, and has been teaching
and refining her methods for two decades.

Also by Julia Cameron

The Artist's Way

A Spiritual Path to Higher Creativity

Julia Cameron

MACMILLAN

This sourcebook is dedicated to Mark Bryan.
Mark urged me to write it, helped shape it, and co-taught it.
Without him it would not exist.

First published in the UK 1994 by Souvenir Press Ltd

This edition published 2016 by Macmillan
an imprint of Pan Macmillan
20 New Wharf Road, London N1 9RR
Associated companies throughout the world
www.panmacmillan.com

ISBN 978-1-5098-2947-7

9 8 7 6 5

A CIP catalogue record for this book is available from the British Library.

Printed and bound by CPI Group (UK) Ltd, Croydon, CR0 4YY

Visit **www.panmacmillan.com** to read more about all our books
and to buy them. You will also find features, author interviews and
news of any author events, and you can sign up for e-newsletters
so that you're always first to hear about our new releases.

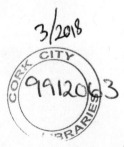

CONTENTS

PREFACE

I AM SEATED ALONE in a cafe, dining solo. A woman approaches my table.

"Pardon me," she says, "has anyone ever told you you resemble Julia Cameron?"

Startled, I reply, "I *am* Julia Cameron."

Now it is the woman's turn to be surprised.

"Oh my God," she exclaims, "your book changed my life. It made me a novelist."

"That's wonderful," I tell her, genuinely pleased.

"I bet you hear stories like mine all the time," the woman says.

"In fact, I do, but it doesn't take away the thrill."

Twenty-five years ago, I published *The Artist's Way*, a book that I think of as a support kit for artists. Its popularity caught me by surprise. I thought I was writing a book for myself and a handful of friends. Instead, I wrote a book that spoke to millions. It had a central premise—we are all creative—and with the use of a few simple tools, we can all become more creative.

Creativity, I believed, was a spiritual practice. We had only to open ourselves up to the Great Creator working through us. We became channels for spiritual energy to enter the world. Writing, painting, dancing, acting—no matter what form our creativity took, the Great Creator caused us to flourish. And so, encounters like mine in the cafe became commonplace.

The sentence is always the same: "Your book changed my life."

"No," I often reply. "You changed your life. You used the tools I laid out for you."

I think it is important for people to own their own spiritual practice. My toolkit is simple, and it invites practitioners to embrace simplicity. A recent review of my latest book noted that the tools were "simple and repetitive." I think of this as a good thing. The tools do not change book to book. The same simple tools that worked in *The Artist's Way* work still, a dozen books later.

In my travels, I encounter practitioners who have used the tools for years. "I've done Morning Pages for fifteen years," a man recently told me. His Morning Pages—three pages of longhand, morning writing, have filled journal after journal. He doesn't give them up, because they "work."

A woman tells me the second primary tool, Artist Dates, a once a week, festive, solo expedition, have given her a life of adventure.

Used together, Morning Pages and Artist Dates do transform lives.

"I've given your book to my mother and my sister," a woman tells me at a book signing. "It worked for all of us," she says. "Now I want you to sign a book for my boyfriend."

I ask his name, and write the simple phrase, "May our words be friends."

I trust that the book will "work" for him, too. I have come to rely on the book. I trust that it is indeed life-changing.

"Julia, don't you get tired of hearing our stories?" I am asked. The answer is no. Creativity is never tiresome. It is always an adventure, one I have been privileged to share.

"I was a very unhappy lawyer," a Broadway actor tells me. "Then I used your tools. Now I am an actor—and a happy one."

"I was what you called a 'shadow artist,'" a thriving director tells me. "I was a producer until I used your toolkit, and emerged as a director. I've worked with your book three times, and each time has led to a breakthrough. Thank you."

"Your tools felt natural to me," a fine arts photographer tells me. "I used to create in spurts, but your tools have given me consistent productivity."

"Before using *The Artist's Way*, my life was very dramatic," a poet tells me. "I was always waiting for inspiration to strike like lightning. Now I know that my creativity is a steady flow. I write poems regularly, and without high drama. The poems I write are just as good as any I wrote before."

Sentiments like these make my years of teaching worthwhile. I am delighted to have been of service. I receive heartfelt letters thanking me for my work and telling me of the changes it has wrought.

Occasionally, the thank-yous are more public. Novelist Patricia Cornwell thanked me in the dedication of her thriller *Trace*. Musician Pete Townsend cited *The Artist's Way* in his autobiography *Who Am I*. While it is thrilling to have celebrity endorsements, the book is perhaps at its best helping the lesser-knowns—and the help isn't restricted to creativity issues.

"Julia, I was drunk in the outback. Now I'm sober, and a Hollywood screenwriter," one practitioner wrote me. It is not uncommon for users of the pages to face down difficult issues such as sobriety, childhood trauma, and obesity. The pages urge honesty in facing down demons.

Last fall I taught a class of ninety people in Sedona. On the second night, a meeting was convened for all who felt the impact of *The Artist's Way* on their well-being. Person after person cited breakthroughs to clarity and health. When it was my turn to share, I told the group that their recovery gave me great pride. I was grateful for their acknowledgement; grateful, too, for the many and varied strides they had taken toward mental, physical, and spiritual health.

"Julia," I am sometimes asked, "aren't you afraid you are unblocking a lot of bad art?"

"No," I reply. The opposite seems to be the case. The unblocked art is often very fine, and I find myself thinking, "how could they have not known they were an artist?" And yet, many people do not know until they encounter my book.

Many artists have never received critical early encouragement. As a result, they may not know they are artists at all. Artists love other artists. Shadow artists are gravitating to their rightful tribe, but cannot yet claim their birthright. I urge them to step forward out of the shadows and into the sunlight of creativity.

Most of the time, when we are blocked in an area of our life, it is because we feel safer that way. The toolkit lends practitioners a sense of safety. As they learn to take small risks in their Morning Pages, they are led to larger risks. A step at a time, they emerge as artists. It has been a quarter of a century since the tools were first published. It gives me great satisfaction that the book continues to sell, and sell well. It reinforces my belief that we are all creative and have a hunger for further creativity.

Julia Cameron, 2016

INTRODUCTION

WHEN PEOPLE ASK ME what I do, I usually answer, "I'm a writer-director and I teach these creativity workshops."

The last one interests them.

"How can you teach creativity?" they want to know. Defiance fights with curiosity on their faces.

"I can't," I tell them. "I teach people to *let* themselves be creative."

"Oh. You mean we're all creative?" Now disbelief and hope battle it out.

"Yes."

"You *really* believe that?"

"Yes."

"So what do you do?"

The primary imagination I hold to be the Living Power.

SAMUEL TAYLOR COLERIDGE

This book is what I do. For a decade now, I have taught a spiritual workshop aimed at freeing people's creativity. I have taught artists and nonartists, painters and filmmakers and homemakers and lawyers—anyone interested in living more creatively through practicing an art; even more broadly, anyone interested in practicing the art of creative living. While using, teaching, and sharing tools I have found, devised, divined, and been handed, I have seen blocks dissolved and lives transformed by the simple process of engaging the Great Creator in discovering and recovering our creative powers.

"The Great Creator? That sounds like some Native American god. That sounds too Christian, too New Age, too . . ." Stupid? Simple-minded? Threatening? . . . I know. Think of it as an exercise in open-mindedness. Just think, "Okay, Great Creator, *whatever that is,*" and keep reading. Allow yourself to experiment with the idea there might be a Great Creator and you might get some kind of use from it in freeing your own creativity.

Because *The Artist's Way* is, in essence, a spiritual path, initiated and practiced through creativity, this book uses the word *God.* This may be volatile for some of you—conjuring old, unworkable, unpleasant, or simply unbelievable ideas about God as you were raised to understand "him." Please be open-minded.

Man is asked to make of himself what he is supposed to become to fulfill his destiny.

PAUL TILLICH

I myself do nothing. The Holy Spirit accomplishes all through me.

WILLIAM BLAKE

Remind yourself that to succeed in this course, no god concept is necessary. In fact, many of our commonly held god concepts get in the way. Do not allow semantics to become one more block for you.

When the word *God* is used in these pages, you may substitute the thought *good orderly direction* or *flow.* What we are talking about is a creative energy. *God* is useful shorthand for many of us, but so is *Goddess, Mind, Universe, Source,* and *Higher Power.* . . . The point is not what you name it. The point is that you try using it. For many of us, thinking of it as a form of spiritual electricity has been a very useful jumping-off place.

By the simple, scientific approach of experimentation and observation, a workable connection with the flow of good orderly direction can easily be established. It is not the intent of these pages to engage in explaining, debating, or defining that flow. You do not need to understand electricity to use it.

Do not call it God unless that is comfortable for you. There seems to be no need to name it unless that name is a useful shorthand for what you experience. Do not pretend to believe when you do not. If you remain forever an atheist, agnostic—so be it. You will still be able to experience an altered life through working with these principles.

I have worked artist-to-artist with potters, photographers, poets, screenwriters, dancers, novelists, actors, directors—and with those who knew only what they dreamed to be or who only dreamed of being somehow more creative. I have seen blocked painters paint, broken poets speak in tongues, halt and lame and maimed writers racing through final drafts. I have come to not only believe but know:

No matter what your age or your life path, whether making art is your career or your hobby or your dream, it is not too late or too egotistical or too selfish or too silly to work on your creativity. One fifty-year-old student who "always wanted to write" used these tools and emerged as a prize-winning playwright. A judge used these tools to fulfill his lifelong dreams of sculpting. Not all students become full-time artists as a result of the course. In fact, many full-time artists report that they have become more creatively rounded into full-time people.

Through my own experience—and that of countless others that I have shared—I have come to believe that creativity is our true nature, that blocks are an unnatural thwarting of a process at once as normal and as miraculous as the blossoming of a flower at the end of a slender green stem. I have found this process of making spiritual contact to be both simple and straightforward.

If you are creatively blocked—and I believe all of us are to some extent—it is possible, even probable, that you can learn to create more freely through your willing use of the tools this book provides. Just as doing Hatha Yoga stretches alters consciousness when all you are doing is stretching, doing the exercises in this book alters consciousness when "all" you are doing is writing and playing. Do these things and a breakthrough will follow—whether you believe in it or not. Whether you call *it* a spiritual awakening or not.

In short, the theory doesn't matter as much as the practice itself does. What you are doing is creating pathways in your consciousness through which the creative forces can operate. Once you agree to clearing these pathways, your creativity emerges. In a sense, your creativity is like your blood. Just as blood is a fact of your physical body and nothing you invented, creativity is a fact of your spiritual body and nothing that you must invent.

Why indeed must "God" be a noun? Why not a verb . . . the most active and dynamic of all?

MARY DALY
THEOLOGIAN

MY OWN JOURNEY

I began teaching the creativity workshops in New York. I taught them because I was *told* to teach them. One minute I was walking in the West Village on a cobblestone street with beautiful afternoon light. The next minute I suddenly knew that I should begin teaching people, groups of people, how to unblock. Maybe it was a wish exhaled on somebody else's walk. Certainly Greenwich Village must contain a greater density of artists—blocked and otherwise—than nearly anyplace else in America.

"I need to unblock," someone may have breathed out.

"I know how to do it," I may have responded, picking up the cue. My life has always included strong internal directives. *Marching orders,* I call them.

In any case, I suddenly knew that I did know how to un-block people and that I was meant to do so, starting then and there with the lessons I myself had learned.

Where did the lessons come from?

In 1978, in January, I stopped drinking. I had never thought drinking made me a writer, but now I suddenly thought not drinking might make me stop. In my mind, drinking and writing went together like, well, scotch and soda. For me, the trick was always getting past the fear and onto the page. I was playing beat the clock—trying to write before the booze closed in like fog and my window of creativity was blocked again.

In the brush doing what it's doing, it will stumble on what one couldn't do by oneself.

ROBERT MOTHERWELL

By the time I was thirty and abruptly sober, I had an office on the Paramount lot and had made a whole career out of that kind of creativity. Creative in spasms. Creative as an act of will and ego. Creative on behalf of others. Creative, yes, but in spurts, like blood from a severed carotid artery. A decade of writing and all I knew was how to make these headlong dashes and hurl myself, against all odds, at the wall of whatever I was writing. If creativity was spiritual in any sense, it was only in its resemblance to a crucifixion. I fell upon the thorns of prose. I bled.

If I could have continued writing the old, painful way, I would certainly still be doing it. The week I got sober, I had two national magazine pieces out, a newly minted feature script, and an alcohol problem I could not handle any longer.

I told myself that if sobriety meant no creativity I did not want to be sober. Yet I recognized that drinking would kill me *and* the creativity. I needed to learn to write sober—or else give up writing entirely. Necessity, not virtue, was the beginning of my spirituality. I was forced to find a new creative path. And that is where my lessons began.

I learned to turn my creativity over to the only god I could believe in, the god of creativity, the life force Dylan Thomas called "the force that through the green fuse drives the flower." I learned to get out of the way and let that creative force work through me. I learned to just show up at the page and write down what I heard. Writing became more like eavesdropping and less like inventing a nuclear bomb. It wasn't so tricky, and it didn't blow up on me anymore. I didn't have to be in the mood.

I didn't have to take my emotional temperature to see if inspiration was pending. I simply wrote. No negotiations. Good, bad? None of my business. *I* wasn't doing it. By resigning as the self-conscious author, I wrote freely.

In retrospect, I am astounded I could let go of the drama of being a suffering artist. Nothing dies harder than a bad idea. And few ideas are worse than the ones we have about art. We can charge so many things off to our suffering-artist identity: drunkenness, promiscuity, fiscal problems, a certain ruthlessness or self-destructiveness in matters of the heart. We all know how broke-crazy-promiscuous-unreliable artists are. And if they don't have to be, then what's my excuse?

The position of the artist is humble. He is essentially a channel.

PIET MONDRIAN

The idea that I could be sane, sober, and creative terrified me, implying, as it did, the possibility of personal accountability. "You mean if I have these gifts, I'm supposed to use them?" Yes.

Providentially, I was sent another blocked writer to work with—and on—at this time. I began to teach him what I was learning. (Get out of the way. Let *it* work through you. Accumulate pages, not judgments.) He, too, began to unblock. Now there were two of us. Soon I had another "victim," this one a painter. The tools worked for visual artists, too.

This was very exciting to me. In my grander moments, I imagined I was turning into a creative cartographer, mapping a way out of confusion for myself and for whoever wanted to follow. I *never* planned to become a teacher. I was only angry I'd never had a teacher myself. Why did I have to learn what I learned the way I learned it: all by trial and error, all by walking into walls? We artists should be more teachable, I thought. Shortcuts and hazards of the trail could be flagged.

These were the thoughts that eddied with me as I took my afternoon walks—enjoying the light off the Hudson, plotting what I would write next. Enter the marching orders: I was to teach.

Within a week, I was offered a teaching position and space at the New York Feminist Art Institute—which I had never heard of. My first class—blocked painters, novelists, poets, and filmmakers—assembled itself. I began teaching them the lessons that are now in this book. Since that class there have been many others, and many more lessons as well.

God must become an activity in our consciousness.

JOEL S. GOLDSMITH

The Artist's Way began as informal class notes mandated by my partner, Mark Bryan. As word of mouth spread, I began mailing out packets of materials. A peripatetic Jungian, John Giannini, spread word of the techniques wherever he lectured—seemingly everywhere. Requests for materials always followed. Next, the creation spirituality network got word of the work, and people wrote in from Dubuque, British Columbia, Indiana. Students materialized all over the globe. "I am in Switzerland with the State Department. Please send me . . ." So I did.

The packets expanded and the number of students expanded. Finally, as the result of some *very* pointed urging from Mark—"Write it *all* down. You can help a lot of people. It should be a *book*"—I began formally to assemble my thoughts. I wrote and Mark, who was by this time my co-teacher and taskmaster, told me what I had left out. I wrote more and Mark told me what I had *still* left out. He reminded me that I had seen plenty of miracles to support my theories and urged me to include those, too. I put on the page what I had been putting into practice for a decade.

The resulting pages emerged as a blueprint for do-it-yourself recovery. Like mouth-to-mouth resuscitation or the Heimlich maneuver, the tools in this book are intended as life-savers. Please use them and pass them on.

Many times, I've heard words to this effect: "Before I took your class, I was completely separate from my creativity. The years of bitterness and loss had taken their toll. Then, gradually, the miracle started to happen. I have gone back to school to get my degree in theater, I'm auditioning for the first time in years, I'm writing on a steady basis—and, most important of all, I finally feel comfortable calling myself an artist."

I doubt I can convey to you the feeling of the miraculous that I experience as a teacher, witnessing the before and after in the lives of students. Over the duration of the course, the sheer physical transformation can be startling, making me realize that the term *enlightenment* is a literal one. Students' faces often take on a glow as they contact their creative energies. The same charged spiritual atmosphere that fills a great work of art can fill a creativity class. In a sense, as we are creative beings, our lives become our work of art.

Spiritual Electricity
The Basic Principles

FOR MOST OF US, the idea that the creator encourages creativity is a radical thought. We tend to think, or at least fear, that creative dreams are egotistical, something that God wouldn't approve of for us. After all, our creative artist is an inner youngster and prone to childish thinking. If our mom or dad expressed doubt or disapproval for our creative dreams, we may project that same attitude onto a parental god. This thinking must be undone.

What we are talking about is an induced—or invited—spiritual experience. I refer to this process as *spiritual chiropractic.* We undertake certain spiritual exercises to achieve alignment with the creative energy of the universe.

If you think of the universe as a vast electrical sea in which you are immersed and from which you are formed, opening to your creativity changes you from something bobbing in that sea to a more fully functioning, more conscious, more cooperative part of that ecosystem.

As a teacher, I often sense the presence of something transcendent—a spiritual electricity, if you will—and I have come to rely on it in transcending my own limitations. I take the phrase *inspired teacher* to be a quite literal compliment. A higher hand than just my own engages us. Christ said, "Wherever two or more are gathered together, there I am in your midst." The god of creativity seems to feel the same way.

The heart of creativity is an experience of the mystical union; the heart of the mystical union is an experience of creativity. Those who speak in spiritual terms routinely refer to God as the creator but seldom see *creator* as the literal term for *artist*. I am suggesting you take the term *creator* quite literally. You are seeking to forge a creative alliance, artist-to-artist with the Great Creator. Accepting this concept can greatly expand your creative possibilities.

As you work with the tools in this book, as you undertake the weekly tasks, many changes will be set in motion. Chief among these changes will be the triggering of *synchronicity:* we change and the universe furthers and expands that change. I have an irreverent shorthand for this that I keep taped to my writing desk: "Leap, and the net will appear."

It is my experience both as an artist and as a teacher that when we move out on faith into the act of creation, the universe is able to advance. It is a little like opening the gate at the top of a field irrigation system. Once we remove the blocks, the flow moves in.

Again, I do not ask you to *believe* this. In order for this creative emergence to happen, you don't have to believe in God. I simply ask you to observe and note this process as it unfolds. In effect, you will be midwiving and witnessing your own creative progression.

Creativity is an experience—to my eye, a spiritual experience. It does not matter which way you think of it: creativity leading to spirituality or spirituality leading to creativity. In fact, I do not make a distinction between the two. In the face of such experience, the whole question of belief is rendered obsolete. As Carl Jung answered the question of belief late in his life, "I don't believe; I know."

The following spiritual principles are the bedrock on which creative recovery and discovery can be built. Read them through once a day, and keep an inner ear cocked for any shifts in attitudes or beliefs.

The music of this opera [Madame Butterfly] was dictated to me by God; I was merely instrumental in putting it on paper and communicating it to the public.

GIACOMO PUCCINI

Straightaway the ideas flow in upon me, directly from God.

JOHANNES BRAHMS

We must accept that this creative pulse within us is God's creative pulse itself.

JOSEPH CHILTON PEARCE

It is the creative potential itself in human beings that is the image of God.

MARY DALY

BASIC PRINCIPLES

1. Creativity is the natural order of life. Life is energy: pure creative energy.

2. There is an underlying, in-dwelling creative force infusing all of life—including ourselves.

3. When we open ourselves to our creativity, we open ourselves to the creator's creativity within us and our lives.

4. We are, ourselves, creations. And we, in turn, are meant to continue creativity by being creative ourselves.

5. Creativity is God's gift to us. Using our creativity is our gift back to God.

6. The refusal to be creative is self-will and is counter to our true nature.

7. When we open ourselves to exploring our creativity, we open ourselves to God: good orderly direction.

8. As we open our creative channel to the creator, many gentle but powerful changes are to be expected.

9. It is safe to open ourselves up to greater and greater creativity.

10. Our creative dreams and yearnings come from a divine source. As we move toward our dreams, we move toward our divinity.

Every blade of grass has its Angel that bends over it and whispers, "Grow, grow."

THE TALMUD

Great improvisors are like priests. They are thinking only of their god.

STÉPHANE GRAPPELLI
MUSICIAN

What we play is life.

LOUIS ARMSTRONG

Creativity is harnessing universality and making it flow through your eyes.

PETER KOESTENBAUM

I paint not by sight but by faith. Faith gives you sight.

AMOS FERGUSON

Why should we all use our creative power . . . ? Because there is nothing that makes people so generous, joyful, lively, bold and compassionate, so indifferent to fighting and the accumulation of objects and money.

BRENDA UELAND

HOW TO USE THIS BOOK
FOR YOUR CREATIVE RECOVERY

There are a number of ways to use this book. Most of all, I invite you to use it creatively. This section offers you a sort of road map through the process, with some specific ideas about how to proceed. Some students have done the course solo; others have formed circles to work through the book together. (In the back of the book, you'll find guidelines about doing the work in groups.) No matter which way you choose, *The Artist's Way* will work for you.

First, you may want to glance through the book to get a sense of the territory covered. (Reading the book through is not the same as using it.) Each chapter includes essays, exercises, tasks, and a weekly check-in. Don't be daunted by the amount of work it seems to entail. Much of the work is really play, and the course takes little more than one hour a day.

When I am formally teaching, I suggest students set a weekly schedule. For example, if you're going to work a Sunday-to-Sunday week, begin by reading the chapter of the week on Sunday night. After you've read the chapter, speed-write through the exercises. The exercises in each week are critical. So are the morning pages and the artist date. (More about these in the next chapter.) You probably won't have time to complete all of the other tasks in any given week. Try to do about half. Know that the rest are there for use when you are able to get back to them. In choosing which half of the tasks to do, use two guidelines. Pick those that appeal to you and those you strongly resist. Leave the more neutral ones for later. Just remember, in choosing, that we often resist what we most need.

In all, make a time commitment of about seven to ten hours a week—an hour a day, or slightly more if you choose. This modest commitment to using the tools can yield tremendous results within the twelve weeks of the course. The same tools, used over a longer period, can alter the trajectory of a lifetime.

In working with this book, remember that *The Artist's Way* is a spiral path. You will circle through some of the issues over and over, each time at a different level. There is no such thing as being done with an artistic life. Frustrations and rewards exist at all levels on the path. Our aim here is to find the trail, establish our footing, and begin the climb. The creative vistas that open will quickly excite you.

What to Expect

Many of us wish we were more creative. Many of us sense we *are* more creative, but unable to effectively tap that creativity. Our dreams elude us. Our lives feel somehow flat. Often, we have great ideas, wonderful dreams, but are unable to actualize them for ourselves. Sometimes we have specific creative longings we would love to be able to fulfill—learning to play the piano, painting, taking an acting class, or writing. Sometimes our goal is more diffuse. We hunger for what might be called creative living—an expanded sense of creativity in our business lives, in sharing with our children, our spouse, our friends.

While there is no quick fix for instant, pain-free creativity, creative recovery (or discovery) is a teachable, trackable spiritual process. Each of us is complex and highly individual, yet there are common recognizable denominators to the creative recovery process.

Working with this process, I see a certain amount of defiance and giddiness in the first few weeks. This entry stage is followed closely by explosive anger in the course's midsection. The anger is followed by grief, then alternating waves of resistance and hope. This peaks-and-valleys phase of growth becomes a series of expansions and contractions, a birthing process in which students experience intense elation and defensive skepticism.

This choppy growth phase is followed by a strong urge to abandon the process and return to life as we know it. In other words, a bargaining period. People are often tempted to abandon the course at this point. I call this a creative U-turn. Recommitment to the process next triggers the free-fall of a major ego surrender. Following this, the final phase of the course is characterized by a new sense of self marked by increased

The purpose of art is not a rarified, intellectual distillate—it is life, intensified, brilliant life.

ALAIN ARIAS-MISSON

What lies behind us and what lies before us are tiny matters, compared to what lies within us.

RALPH WALDO
EMERSON

autonomy, resilience, expectancy, and excitement—as well as by the capacity to make and execute concrete creative plans.

If this sounds like a lot of emotional tumult, it is. When we engage in a creativity recovery, we enter into a withdrawal process from life as we know it. *Withdrawal* is another way of saying *detachment* or *nonattachment,* which is emblematic of consistent work with any meditation practice.

In movie terms, we slowly *pull focus,* lifting up and away from being embedded in our lives until we attain an overview. This overview empowers us to make valid creative choices. Think of it as a journey with difficult, varied, and fascinating terrain. You are moving to higher ground. The fruit of your withdrawal is what you need to understand as a positive process, both painful and exhilarating.

Many of us find that we have squandered our own creative energies by investing disproportionately in the lives, hopes, dreams, and plans of others. Their lives have obscured and detoured our own. As we consolidate a core through our withdrawal process, we become more able to articulate our own boundaries, dreams, and authentic goals. Our personal flexibility increases while our malleability to the whims of others decreases. We experience a heightened sense of autonomy and possibility.

Ordinarily, when we speak of withdrawal, we think of having a substance removed from us. We give up alcohol, drugs, sugar, fats, caffeine, nicotine—and we suffer a withdrawal. It's useful to view creative withdrawal a little differently. We ourselves are the substance we withdraw *to,* not from, as we pull our overextended and misplaced creative energy back into our own core.

We begin to excavate our buried dreams. This is a tricky process. Some of our dreams are very volatile, and the mere act of brushing them off sends an enormous surge of energy bolting through our denial system. Such grief! Such loss! Such pain! It is at this point in the recovery process that we make what Robert Bly calls a "descent into ashes." We mourn the self we abandoned. We greet this self as we might greet a lover at the end of a long and costly war.

To effect a creative recovery, we must undergo a time of

mourning. In dealing with the suicide of the "nice" self we have been making do with, we find a certain amount of grief to be essential. Our tears prepare the ground for our future growth. Without this creative moistening, we may remain barren. We must allow the bolt of pain to strike us. Remember, this is useful pain; lightning illuminates.

How do you know if you are creatively blocked? Jealousy is an excellent clue. Are there artists whom you resent? Do you tell yourself, "I could do that, if only . . ." Do you tell yourself that if only you took your creative potential seriously, you might:

- Stop telling yourself, "It's too late."

- Stop waiting until you make enough money to do something you'd really love.

- Stop telling yourself, "It's just my ego" whenever you yearn for a more creative life.

- Stop telling yourself that dreams don't matter, that they are only dreams and that you should be more sensible.

- Stop fearing that your family and friends would think you crazy.

- Stop telling yourself that creativity is a luxury and that you should be grateful for what you've got.

As you learn to recognize, nurture, and protect your inner artist, you will be able to move beyond pain and creative constriction. You will learn ways to recognize and resolve fear, remove emotional scar tissue, and strengthen your confidence. Damaging old ideas about creativity will be explored and discarded. Working with this book, you will experience an intensive, guided encounter with your own creativity—your private villains, champions, wishes, fears, dreams, hopes, and triumphs. The experience will make you excited, depressed, angry, afraid, joyous, hopeful, and, ultimately, more free.

The Basic Tools

THERE ARE TWO PIVOTAL tools in creative recovery: *the morning pages* and *the artist date*. A lasting creative awakening requires the consistent use of both. I like to introduce them both immediately, and at sufficient length to answer most of your questions. This chapter explains these tools carefully and in depth. Please read it with special care and begin the immediate use of both tools.

THE MORNING PAGES

In order to retrieve your creativity, you need to find it. I ask you to do this by an apparently pointless process I call *the morning pages*. You will do the pages daily through all the weeks of the course and, I hope, much longer. I have been doing them for a decade now. I have students who have worked with them nearly that long and who would no more abandon them than breathing.

Ginny, a writer-producer, credits the morning pages with inspiration for her recent screenplays and clarity in planning her network specials. "I'm superstitious about them by now," she says. "When I was editing my last special, I would get up at 5:00 A.M. to get them done before I went in to work."

What are morning pages? Put simply, the morning pages

are three pages of longhand writing, strictly stream-of-consciousness: "Oh, god, another morning. I have NOTHING to say. I need to wash the curtains. Did I get my laundry yesterday? Blah, blah, blah . . ." They might also, more ingloriously, be called *brain drain,* since that is one of their main functions.

There is no wrong way to do morning pages. These daily morning meanderings are not meant to be *art.* Or even *writing.* I stress that point to reassure the nonwriters working with this book. Writing is simply one of the tools. Pages are meant to be, simply, the act of moving the hand across the page and writing down *whatever* comes to mind. Nothing is too petty, too silly, too stupid, or too weird to be included.

The morning pages are not supposed to sound smart— although sometimes they might. Most times they won't, and nobody will ever know except you. Nobody is allowed to read your morning pages except you. And you shouldn't even read them yourself for the first eight weeks or so. Just write three pages, and stick them into an envelope. Or write three pages in a spiral notebook and don't leaf back through. *Just write three pages* . . . and write three more pages the next day.

> September 30, 1991 . . . Over the weekend, for Domenica's biology project, she and I went bug hunting on the Rio Grande and Pott Creek. We collected water crawlies and butterflies. I made a crimson homemade butterfly net that was quite functional although dragonflies eluded us to our dismay. We did not catch the tarantula strolling down the dirt road near our house. We just enjoyed spotting it.

Although occasionally colorful, the morning pages are often negative, frequently fragmented, often self-pitying, repetitive, stilted or babyish, angry or bland—even silly sounding. Good!

> Oct. 2, 1991 . . . I am up and have had a headache and have taken aspirin and feel a little better although still shaky. I may have that flu after all. I am getting to the bot-

---

Words are a form of action, capable of influencing change.

INGRID BENGIS

You need to claim the events of your life to make yourself yours.

ANNE-WILSON SCHAEF

tom of a lot of unpacking and still no teapot from Laura whom I am sorely missing. What a heartbreak . . .

All that angry, whiny, petty stuff that you write down in the morning stands between you and your creativity. Worrying about the job, the laundry, the funny knock in the car, the weird look in your lover's eye—this stuff eddies through our subconscious and muddies our days. Get it on the page.

The morning pages are the primary tool of creative recovery. As blocked artists, we tend to criticize ourselves mercilessly. Even if we look like functioning artists to the world, we feel we never do enough and what we do isn't right. We are victims of our own internalized perfectionist, a nasty internal and eternal critic, the Censor, who resides in our (left) brain and keeps up a constant stream of subversive remarks that are often disguised as the truth. The Censor says wonderful things like: "You call that writing? What a joke. You can't even punctuate. If you haven't done it by now you never will. You can't even spell. What makes you think you can be creative?" And on and on.

Make this a rule: always remember that your Censor's negative opinions are not the truth. This takes practice. By spilling out of bed and straight onto the page every morning, you learn to evade the Censor. Because there is no wrong way to write the morning pages, the Censor's opinion doesn't count.

Let your Censor rattle on. (And it will.) Just keep your hand moving across the page. Write down the Censor's thoughts if you want to. Note how it loves to aim for your creative jugular. Make no mistake: the Censor is out to get you. It's a cunning foe. Every time you get smarter, so does it. So you wrote one good play? The Censor tells you that's all there is. So you drew your first sketch? The Censor says, "It's not Picasso."

Think of your Censor as a cartoon serpent, slithering around your creative Eden, hissing vile things to keep you off guard. If a serpent doesn't appeal to you, you might want to find a good cartoon image of your Censor, maybe the shark from *Jaws,* and put an *X* through it. Post it where you tend to write or on the inside cover of your notebook. Just making the Censor into the nasty, clever little character that it is begins to pry loose some of its power over you and your creativity.

A mind too active is no mind at all.

THEODORE ROETHKE

The events in our lives happen in a sequence in time, but in their significance to ourselves, they find their own order . . . the continuous thread of revelation.

EUDORA WELTY

More than one student has tacked up an unflattering picture of the parent responsible for the Censor's installation in his or her psyche and called that his or her Censor. The point is to stop taking the Censor as the voice of reason and learn to hear it for the blocking device that it is. Morning pages will help you to do this.

Morning pages are nonnegotiable. Never skip or skimp on morning pages. Your mood doesn't matter. The rotten thing your Censor says doesn't matter. We have this idea that we need to be in the mood to write. We don't.

Morning pages will teach you that your mood doesn't really matter. Some of the best creative work gets done on the days when you feel that everything you're doing is just plain junk. The morning pages will teach you to stop judging and just let yourself write. So what if you're tired, crabby, distracted, stressed? Your artist is a child and it needs to be fed. Morning pages feed your artist child. So write your morning pages.

Three pages of whatever crosses your mind—that's all there is to it. If you can't think of anything to write, then write, "I can't think of anything to write. . . ." Do this until you have filled three pages. *Do anything until you have filled three pages.*

When people ask, "Why do we write morning pages?" I joke, "To get to the other side." They think I am kidding, but I'm not. Morning pages do get us to the other side: the other side of our fear, of our negativity, of our moods. Above all, they get us beyond our Censor. Beyond the reach of the Censor's babble we find our own quiet center, the place where we hear the still, small voice that is at once our creator's and our own.

A word is in order here about logic brain and artist brain. *Logic brain* is our brain of choice in the Western Hemisphere. It is the categorical brain. It thinks in a neat, linear fashion. As a rule, logic brain perceives the world according to known categories. A horse is a certain combination of animal parts that make up a horse. A fall forest is viewed as a series of colors that add up to "fall forest." It looks at a fall forest and notes: red, orange, yellow, green, gold.

Logic brain was and is our survival brain. It works on

known principles. Anything unknown is perceived as wrong and possibly dangerous. Logic brain likes things to be neat little soldiers marching in a straight line. Logic brain is the brain we usually listen to, especially when we are telling ourselves to be sensible.

Logic brain is our Censor, our second (and third and fourth) thoughts. Faced with an original sentence, phrase, paint squiggle, it says, "What the hell is that? That's not right!"

Artist brain is our inventor, our child, our very own personal absent-minded professor. Artist brain says, "Hey! That is so neat!" It puts odd things together (boat equals wave and walker). It likes calling a speeding GTO a wild animal: "The black howling wolf pulled into the drive-in . . ."

Artist brain is our creative, holistic brain. It thinks in patterns and shadings. It sees a fall forest and thinks: Wow! Leaf bouquet! Pretty! Gold-gilt-shimmery-earthskin-king's-carpet! Artist brain is associative and freewheeling. It makes new connections, yoking together images to invoke meaning: like the Norse myths calling a boat "wave-horse." In *Star Wars,* the name Skywalker is a lovely artist-brain flash.

Why all this logic-brain/artist-brain talk? Because the morning pages teach logic brain to stand aside and let artist brain play.

The Censor is part of our leftover survival brain. It was the part in charge of deciding whether it was safe for us to leave the forest and go out into the meadow. Our Censor scans our creative meadow for any dangerous beasties. Any original thought can look pretty dangerous to our Censor.

The only sentences/paintings/sculptures/photographs it likes are ones that it has seen many times before. Safe sentences. Safe paintings. Not exploratory blurts, squiggles, or jottings. Listen to your Censor and it will tell you that everything original is wrong/dangerous/rotten.

Who wouldn't be blocked if every time you tiptoed into the open somebody (your Censor) made fun of you? The morning pages will teach you to stop listening to that ridicule. They will allow you to detach from your negative Censor.

It may be useful for you to think of the morning pages as meditation. It may not be the practice of meditation you are

Poetry often enters through the window of irrelevance.

M. C. RICHARDS

accustomed to. You may, in fact, not be accustomed to meditating at all. The pages may not seem spiritual or even meditative—more like negative and materialistic, actually—but they are a valid form of meditation that gives us insight and helps us effect change in our lives.

Let's take a look at what we stand to gain by meditating. There are many ways of thinking about meditation. Scientists speak of it in terms of brain hemispheres and shunting techniques. We move from logic brain to artist brain and from fast to slow, shallow to deep. Management consultants, in pursuit of corporate physical health, have learned to think of meditation primarily as a stress-management technique. Spiritual seekers choose to view the process as a gateway to God. Artists and creativity mavens approve of it as a conduit for higher creative insights.

All of these notions are true—as far as they go. They do not go far enough. Yes, we will alter our brain hemisphere, lower our stress, discover an inner contact with a creative source, and have many creative insights. Yes, for any one of these reasons, the pursuit is a worthy one. Even taken in combination, however, they are still intellectual constructs for what is primarily an experience of wholeness, rightness, and power.

We meditate to discover our own identity, our right place in the scheme of the universe. Through meditation, we acquire and eventually acknowledge our connection to an inner power source that has the ability to transform our outer world. In other words, meditation gives us not only the light of insight but also the power for expansive change.

Insight in and of itself is an intellectual comfort. Power in and of itself is a blind force that can destroy as easily as build. It is only when we consciously learn to link power and light that we begin to feel our rightful identities as creative beings. The morning pages allow us to forge this link. They provide us with a spiritual ham-radio set to contact the Creator Within. For this reason, the morning pages are a spiritual practice.

It is impossible to write morning pages for any extended period of time without coming into contact with an unexpected inner power. Although I used them for many years be-

Inspiration may be a form of superconsciousness, or perhaps of subconsciousness—I wouldn't know. But I am sure it is the antithesis of self-consciousness.

AARON COPLAND

fore I realized this, the pages are a pathway to a strong and clear sense of self. They are a trail that we follow into our own interior, where we meet both our own creativity and our creator.

Morning pages map our own interior. Without them, our dreams may remain terra incognita. I know mine did. Using them, the light of insight is coupled with the power for expansive change. It is very difficult to complain about a situation morning after morning, month after month, without being moved to constructive action. The pages lead us out of despair and into undreamed-of solutions.

The first time I did morning pages, I was living in Taos, New Mexico. I had gone there to sort myself out—into what, I didn't know. For the third time in a row, I'd had a film scuttled due to studio politics. Such disasters are routine to screenwriters, but to me they felt like miscarriages. Cumulatively, they were disastrous. I wanted to give the movies up. Movies had broken my heart. I didn't want any more brainchildren to meet untimely deaths. I'd gone to New Mexico to mend my heart and see what else, if anything, I might want to do.

Living in a small adobe house that looked north to Taos Mountain, I began a practice of writing morning pages. Nobody told me to do them. I had never heard of anybody doing them. I just got the insistent, inner sense that I should do them and so I did. I sat at a wooden table looking north to Taos Mountain and I wrote.

The morning pages were my pastime, something to do instead of staring at the mountain all the time. The mountain, a humpbacked marvel different in every weather, raised more questions than I did. Wrapped in clouds one day, dark and wet the next, that mountain dominated my view and my morning pages as well. What did it—or anything—mean? I asked page after page, morning after morning. No answer.

And then, one wet morning, a character named Johnny came strolling into my pages. Without planning to, I was writing a novel. The morning pages had shown me a way.

Anyone who faithfully writes morning pages will be led to a connection with a source of wisdom within. When I am stuck with a painful situation or problem that I don't think I know how to handle, I will go to the pages and ask for

It always comes back to the same necessity: go deep enough and there is a bedrock of truth, however hard.

MAY SARTON

guidance. To do this, I write "LJ" as a shorthand for me, "Little Julie," and then I ask my question.

LJ: What should I tell them about this inner wisdom? (Then I listen for the reply and write that down, too.)

ANSWER: You should tell them everyone has a direct dial to God. No one needs to go through an operator. Tell them to try this technique with a problem of their own. They will.

Sometimes, as above, the answer may seem flippant or too simple. I have come to believe that *seem* is the operative word. Very often, when I act on the advice I have been given, it is exactly right—far more right than something more complicated would have been. And so, for the record, I want to say: pages are my way of meditating; I do them because they work.

A final assurance: the morning pages will work for painters, for sculptors, for poets, for actors, for lawyers, for housewives—for anyone who wants to try anything creative. Don't think they are a tool for writers only. Hooey. These pages are not intended for writers only. Lawyers who use them swear they make them more effective in court. Dancers claim their balance improves—and not just emotionally. If anything, writers, who have a regrettable desire to *write* morning pages instead of just do them, may have the hardest time seeing their impact. What they're likely to see is that their other writing seems to suddenly be far more free and expansive and somehow easy to do. In short, no matter what your reservation or your occupation, morning pages will function for you.

Timothy, a buttoned-down, buttoned-lip curmudgeon millionaire, began writing morning pages with a skeptic's scorn. He didn't want to do them without some proof that they would work. The damn pages had no label, no Dun and Bradstreet rating. They just sounded silly, and Timothy hated silly.

Timothy was, in street parlance, a serious player. His poker face was so straight it looked more like a fireplace poker than a mere cardsharp's defense. Practiced for years in the corporate board room, Timothy's invincible facade was as dark, shiny, and expensive as mahogany. No emotions scratched the surface of this man's calm. He was a one-man monument to the Masculine Mystique.

"Oh, all right . . ." Timothy agreed to the pages, but only because he had paid good money to be told to do them. Within three weeks, straightlaced, pin-striped Timothy became a morning-pages advocate. The results of his work with them convinced him. He started—heaven forbid—to have a little creative fun. "I bought guitar strings for this old guitar I had lying around," he reported one week. And then, "I rewired my stereo. I bought some wonderful Italian recordings." Although he hesitated to acknowledge it, even to himself, Timothy's writer's block was melting. Up at dawn, Gregorian chant on the stereo, he was writing freely.

Not everyone undertakes the morning pages with such obvious antagonism. Phyllis, a leggy, racehorse socialite who for years had hidden her brains behind her beauty and her life behind her man's, tried the morning pages with a great deal of surface cheer—and an inner conviction they would never work for her. It had been ten years since she had allowed herself to write anything other than letters and bread-and-butter lists. About a month into morning pages, seemingly out of nowhere, Phyllis got her first poem. In the three years she has used pages since, she has written poems, speeches, radio shows, and a nonfiction book.

Anton, grumpy but graceful in his use of the pages, accomplished unblocking as an actor. Laura, talented but blocked as a writer, painter, and musician, found that the morning pages moved her to her piano, typewriter, and paint supplies.

While you may undertake this course with an agenda as to what you want unblocked, the tools may free creative areas you have long ignored or even been blind to. Ingeborg, using the pages to unblock her creative writer, moved from being one of Germany's top music critics to composing for the first time in twenty years. She was stunned and made several ecstatic transatlantic calls to share her good news.

Often, the students most resistant to morning pages come to love them the best. In fact, hating the morning pages is a very good sign. Loving them is a good sign, too, if you keep writing even when you suddenly don't. A neutral attitude is the third position, but it's really just a defensive strategy that may mask boredom.

Painting is just another way of keeping a diary.

PABLO PICASSO

Experience, even for a painter, is not exclusively visual.

WALTER MEIGS

Boredom is just "What's the use?" in disguise. And "What's the use?" is fear, and fear means you are secretly in despair. So put your fears on the page. Put anything on the page. Put three pages of it on the page.

THE ARTIST DATE

The other basic tool of *The Artist's Way* may strike you as a nontool, a diversion. You may see clearly how morning pages could work yet find yourself highly dubious about something called an *artist date*. I assure you, artist dates work, too.

Think of this combination of tools in terms of a radio receiver and transmitter. It is a two-step, two-directional process: *out* and then *in*. Doing your morning pages, you are sending—notifying yourself and the universe of your dreams, dissatisfactions, hopes. Doing your artist date, you are receiving—opening yourself to insight, inspiration, guidance.

But what exactly *is* an artist date? An artist date is a block of time, perhaps two hours weekly, especially set aside and committed to nurturing your creative consciousness, your inner artist. In its most primary form, the artist date is an excursion, a play date that you preplan and defend against all interlopers. You do not take anyone on this artist date but you and your inner artist, a.k.a. your creative child. That means no lovers, friends, spouses, children—no taggers-on of any stripe.

If you think this sounds stupid or that you will never be able to afford the time, identify that reaction as resistance. You cannot afford *not* to find time for artist dates.

"Do you spend quality time with each other?" troubled couples are often asked by their therapist. Parents of disturbed children are asked the same thing.

"Well . . . what do you mean, 'quality time'?" is the usual weasely response. "We spend a lot of time together."

"Yes . . . but is it quality time? Do you ever have any fun together?" the therapist may press.

"Fun?" (Whoever heard of having fun in a rotten relationship like this one?)

"Do you go on dates? Just to talk? Just to listen to each other?"

"Dates? . . . But we're married, too busy, too broke, too—"

The most potent muse of all is our own inner child.

STEPHEN
NACHMANOVITCH

At the height of laughter, the universe is flung into a kaleidoscope of new possibilities.

JEAN HOUSTON

"Too scared," the therapist may interrupt. (Hey, don't sugarcoat it.)

It *is* frightening to spend quality time with a child or lover, and our artist can be seen as both to us. A weekly artist date is remarkably threatening—and remarkably productive.

A date? With my artist?

Yes. Your artist needs to be taken out, pampered, and listened to. There are as many ways to evade this commitment as there are days of your life. "I'm too broke" is the favored one, although no one said the date need involve elaborate expenses.

Your artist is a child. Time with a parent matters more than monies spent. A visit to a great junk store, a solo trip to the beach, an old movie seen alone together, a visit to an aquarium or an art gallery—these cost time, not money. Remember, it is the time commitment that is sacred.

In looking for a parallel, think of the child of divorce who gets to see a beloved parent only on weekends. (During most of the week, your artist is in the custody of a stern, workaday adult.) What that child wants is attention, not expensive outings. What that child does not want is to share the precious parent with someone like the new significant other.

Spending time in solitude with your artist child is essential to self-nurturing. A long country walk, a solitary expedition to the beach for a sunrise or sunset, a sortie out to a strange church to hear gospel music, to an ethnic neighborhood to taste foreign sights and sounds—your artist might enjoy any of these. Or your artist might like bowling.

Commit yourself to a weekly artist's date, and then watch your killjoy side try to wriggle out of it. Watch how this sacred time gets easily encroached upon. Watch how the sacred time suddenly includes a third party. Learn to guard against these invasions.

Above all, learn to listen to what your artist child has to say on, and about, these joint expeditions. For example, "Oh, I hate this serious stuff," your artist may exclaim if you persist in taking it only to grown-up places that are culturally edifying and good for it.

Listen to that! It is telling you your art needs more playful inflow. A little fun can go a long way toward making your work feel more like play. We forget that the imagination-at-

The creation of something new is not accomplished by the intellect but by the play instinct acting from inner necessity. The creative mind plays with the objects it loves.

C. G. Jung

Every child is an artist. The problem is how to remain an artist once he grows up.

PABLO PICASSO

During [these] periods of relaxation after concentrated intellectual activity, the intuitive mind seems to take over and can produce the sudden clarifying insights which give so much joy and delight.

FRITJOF CAPRA
PHYSICIST

play is at the heart of all good work. And increasing our capacity for good creative work is what this book is about.

You are likely to find yourself avoiding your artist dates. Recognize this resistance as a fear of intimacy—*self*-intimacy. Often in troubled relationships, we settle into an avoidance pattern with our significant others. We don't want to hear what they are thinking because it just might hurt. So we avoid them, knowing that, once they get the chance, our significant others will probably blurt out something we do not want to hear. It is possible they will want an answer we do not have and can't give them. It is equally possible we might do the same to them and that then the two of us will stare at each other in astonishment, saying, "But I never knew you felt like that!"

It is probable that these self-disclosures, frightening though they are, will lead to the building of a real relationship, one in which the participants are free to be who they are and to become what they wish. This possibility is what makes the risks of self-disclosure and true intimacy profitable. In order to have a real relationship with our creativity, we must take the time and care to cultivate it. Our creativity will use this time to confront us, to confide in us, to bond with us, and to plan.

The morning pages acquaint us with what we think and what we think we need. We identify problem areas and concerns. We complain, enumerate, identify, isolate, fret. This is step one, analogous to prayer. In the course of the release engendered by our artist date, step two, we begin to hear solutions. Perhaps equally important, we begin to fund the creative reserves we will draw on in fulfilling our artistry.

Filling the Well, Stocking the Pond

Art is an image-using system. In order to create, we draw from our inner well. This inner well, an artistic reservoir, is ideally like a well-stocked trout pond. We've got big fish, little fish, fat fish, skinny fish—an abundance of artistic fish to fry. As artists, we must realize that we have to maintain this artistic ecosystem. If we don't give some attention to upkeep, our well is apt to become depleted, stagnant, or blocked.

Any extended period or piece of work draws heavily on

our artistic well. Overtapping the well, like overfishing the pond, leaves us with diminished resources. We fish in vain for the images we require. Our work dries up and we wonder why, "just when it was going so well." The truth is that work can dry up *because* it is going so well.

As artists, we must learn to be self-nourishing. We must become alert enough to consciously replenish our creative resources as we draw on them—to restock the trout pond, so to speak. I call this process *filling the well.*

Filling the well involves the active pursuit of images to refresh our artistic reservoirs. Art is born in attention. Its midwife is detail. Art may seem to spring from pain, but perhaps that is because pain serves to focus our attention onto details (for instance, the excruciatingly beautiful curve of a lost lover's neck). Art may seem to involve broad strokes, grand schemes, great plans. But it is the attention to detail that stays with us; the singular image is what haunts us and becomes art. Even in the midst of pain, this singular image brings delight. The artist who tells you different is lying.

In order to function in the language of art, we must learn to live in it comfortably. The language of art is image, symbol. It is a wordless language even when our very art is to chase it with words. The artist's language is a sensual one, a language of felt experience. When we work at our art, we dip into the well of our experience and scoop out images. Because we do this, we need to learn how to put images back. How do we fill the well?

We feed it images. Art is an artist-brain pursuit. The artist brain is our image brain, home and haven to our best creative impulses. The artist brain cannot be reached—or triggered— effectively by words alone. The artist brain is the sensory brain: sight and sound, smell and taste, touch. These are the elements of magic, and magic is the elemental stuff of art.

In filling the well, think magic. Think delight. Think fun. Do not think duty. Do not do what you *should* do—spiritual sit-ups like reading a dull but recommended critical text. Do what intrigues you, explore what interests you; think mystery, not mastery.

A mystery draws us in, leads us on, lures us. (A duty may

Younger Self—who can be as balky and stubborn as the most cantankerous three-year-old—is not impressed by words. Like a native of Missouri, it wants to be shown. To arouse its interest, we must seduce it with pretty pictures and pleasurable sensations—take it out dining and dancing as it were. Only in this way can Deep Self be reached.

STARHAWK
THEOLOGIAN

Nobody sees a flower—really—it is so small it takes time—we haven't time—and to see takes time, like to have a friend takes time.

GEORGIA O'KEEFFE

So you see, imagination needs moodling—long, inefficient, happy idling, dawdling and puttering.

BRENDA UELAND

numb us out, turn us off, tune us out.) In filling the well, follow your sense of the mysterious, not your sense of what you should know more about. A mystery can be very simple: if I drive this road, not my usual road, what will I see? Changing a known route throws us into the now. We become refocused on the visible, visual world. Sight leads to insight.

A mystery can be simpler even than that: if I light this stick of incense, what will I feel? Scent is an often-overlooked pathway to powerful associations and healing. The scent of Christmas at any time of year—or the scent of fresh bread or homemade soup—can nourish the hungry artist within.

Some sounds lull us. Others stimulate us. Ten minutes of listening to a great piece of music can be a very effective meditation. Five minutes of barefoot dancing to drum music can send our artist into its play-fray-day refreshed.

Filling the well needn't be all novelty. Cooking can fill the well. When we chop and pare vegetables, we do so with our thoughts as well. Remember, art is an artist-brain pursuit. This brain is reached through rhythm—through rhyme, not reason. Scraping a carrot, peeling an apple—these actions are quite literally food for thought.

Any regular, repetitive action primes the well. Writers have heard many woeful tales of the Brontë sisters and poor Jane Austen, forced to hide their stories under their needlework. A little experiment with some mending can cast a whole new light on these activities. Needlework, by definition regular and repetitive, both soothes and stimulates the artist within. Whole plots can be stitched up while we sew. As artists, we can very literally reap what we sew.

"Why do I get my best ideas in the shower?" an exasperated Einstein is said to have remarked. Brain research now tells us that this is because showering is an artist-brain activity.

Showering, swimming, scrubbing, shaving, steering a car—so many *s-like-yes* words!—all of these are regular, repetitive activities that may tip us over from our logic brain into our more creative artist brain. Solutions to sticky creative problems may bubble up through the dishwater, emerge on the freeway just as we are executing a tricky merge, . . .

Learn which of these works best for you and use it. Many

artists have found it useful to keep a notepad or tape recorder next to them as they drive. Steven Spielberg claims that his very best ideas have come to him as he was driving the freeways. This is no accident. Negotiating the flow of traffic, he was an artist immersed in an oncoming, ever-altering flow of images. Images trigger the artist brain. Images fill the well.

Our focused attention is critical to filling the well. We need to encounter our life experiences, not ignore them. Many of us read compulsively to screen our awareness. On a crowded (interesting) train, we train our attention on a newspaper, losing the sights and sounds around us—all images for the well.

The true mystery of the world is the visible, not the invisible.

OSCAR WILDE

CONTRACT

I, _____, understand that I am undertaking an intensive, guided encounter with my own creativity. I commit myself to the twelve-week duration of the course. I, _____, commit to weekly reading, daily morning pages, a weekly artist date, and the fulfillment of each week's tasks.

I, _____, further understand that this course will raise issues and emotions for me to deal with. I, _____, commit myself to excellent self-care—adequate sleep, diet, exercise, and pampering—for the duration of the course.

_____
(signature)

_____
(date)

Artist's block is a very literal expression. Blocks must be acknowledged and dislodged. Filling the well is the surest way to do this.

Art is the imagination at play in the field of time. Let yourself play.

*Inside you there's an artist you
don't know about. . . . Say yes
quickly, if you know, if you've
known it from before the beginning of the universe.*

JALAI UD-DIN RUMI

CREATIVITY CONTRACT

When I am teaching the Artist's Way, I require students to make a contract with themselves, committing to the work of the course. Can you give yourself that gift? Say yes by means of some small ceremony. Buy a nice notebook for your pages; hire your babysitter ahead of time for the weekly artist dates. Read the contract on the preceding page. Amend it, if you like; then sign and date it. Come back to it when you need encouragement to go on.

Recovering a Sense of Safety

This week initiates your creative recovery. You may feel both giddy and defiant, hopeful and skeptical. The readings, tasks, and exercises aim at allowing you to establish a sense of safety, which will enable you to explore your creativity with less fear.

SHADOW ARTISTS

ONE OF OUR CHIEF needs as creative beings is support. Unfortunately, this can be hard to come by. Ideally, we would be nurtured and encouraged first by our nuclear family and then by ever-widening circles of friends, teachers, well-wishers. As young artists, we need and want to be acknowledged for our attempts and efforts as well as for our achievements and triumphs. Unfortunately, many artists never receive this critical early encouragement. As a result, they may not know they are artists at all.

Parents seldom respond, "Try it and see what happens" to artistic urges issuing from their offspring. They offer cautionary advice where support might be more to the point. Timid young artists, adding parental fears to their own, often give up their sunny dreams of artistic careers, settling into the twilight world of could-have-beens and regrets. There, caught between the dream of action and the fear of failure, shadow artists are born.

I am thinking here of Edwin, a miserable millionaire trader whose joy in life comes from his art collection. Strongly

Nothing has a stronger influence psychologically on their environment and especially on their children than the unlived life of the parent.

C. G. JUNG

gifted in the visual arts, he was urged as a child to go into finance. His father bought him a seat on the stock exchange for his twenty-first birthday. He has been a trader ever since. Now in his mid-thirties, he is very rich and very poor. Money cannot buy him creative fulfillment.

Surrounding himself with artists and artifacts, he is like the kid with his nose pressed to the candy-store window. He would love to be more creative but believes that is the prerogative of others, nothing he can aspire to for himself. A generous man, he recently gifted an artist with a year's living expenses so she could pursue her dreams. Raised to believe that the term *artist* could not apply to him, he cannot make that same gift for himself.

Edwin's is not an isolated case. All too often the artistic urges of the artist child are ignored or suppressed. Often with the best intentions, parents try to foster a different, more sensible self for the child. "Stop daydreaming!" is one frequently heard admonition. "You'll never amount to anything if you keep on with you head in the clouds" is another.

Baby artists are urged to think and act like baby doctors or lawyers. A rare family, faced with the myth of the starving artist, tells its children to go right ahead and try for a career in the arts. Instead, if encouraged at all, the children are urged into thinking of the arts as hobbies, creative fluff around the edges of real life.

For many families, a career in the arts exists outside of their social and economic reality: "Art won't pay the electric bill." As a result, if the child is encouraged to consider art in job terms at all, he or she must consider it *sensibly*.

Erin, a gifted children's therapist, was in her mid-thirties before she began experiencing a haunting dissatisfaction in her work. Unsure what direction to take, she began adapting a children's book for the screen. Midway through the adaptation, she suddenly had a telling dream about abandoning her own artist child. Prior to becoming a therapist, she had been a gifted art student. For two decades, she had suppressed her creative urges, pouring all of her creativity into helping others. Now, nearly forty, she found herself longing to help herself.

Erin's story is all too common. Fledgling artists may be encouraged to be art teachers or to specialize in crafts with the handicapped. Young writers may be pushed toward lawyering, a talky, wordy profession, or into medical school because they're so smart. And so the child who is himself a born story-teller may be converted into a gifted therapist who gets his stories secondhand.

Too intimidated to become artists themselves, very often too low in self-worth to even recognize that they have an artistic dream, these people become shadow artists instead. Artists themselves but ignorant of their true identity, shadow artists are to be found shadowing declared artists. Unable to recognize that they themselves may possess the creativity they so admire, they often date or marry people who actively pursue the art career they themselves secretly long for.

I believe that if it were left to artists to choose their own labels, most would choose none.

BEN SHAHN

When Jerry was still blocked as an artist, he began to date Lisa, a gifted but broke free-lance artist. "I am your biggest fan," he often told her. What he did not immediately tell her was that he himself dreamed of being a filmmaker. He had, in fact, an entire library of film books and avidly devoured special-interest magazines on filmmaking. But he was afraid to take steps to actualize his interest. Instead, he poured his time and attention into Lisa and Lisa's art career. Under his guidance, her career flourished. She became solvent and increasingly well known. Jerry remained blocked in his own behalf. When Lisa suggested he take a filmmaking course, he ran for cover. "Not everyone can be an artist," he told her—and himself.

Artists love other artists. Shadow artists are gravitating to their rightful tribe but cannot yet claim their birthright. Very often audacity, not talent, makes one person an artist and another a shadow artist—hiding in the shadows, afraid to step out and expose the dream to the light, fearful that it will disintegrate to the touch.

Shadow artists often choose shadow careers—those close to the desired art, even parallel to it, but not the art itself. Noting their venom, François Truffaut contended that critics were themselves blocked directors, as he had been when he was a critic. He may be right. Intended fiction writers often go into newspapering or advertising, where they can use their gift without taking the plunge into their dreamed-of fiction-writing career. Intended artists may become artist managers and derive a great deal of secondary pleasure from serving their dream even at one remove.

Carolyn, herself a gifted photographer, made a successful but unhappy career as a photographer's rep. Jean, who yearned to write feature films, wrote minimovies in her thirty-second commercial spots. Kelly, who wanted to be a writer but feared taking her creativity seriously, made a profitable career out of repping "really" creative people. Shadow artists all, these women needed to place themselves and their dreams stage center. They knew this, but didn't dare. They had been raised to the role of shadow artist and would need to work consciously to dismantle it.

It takes a great deal of ego strength to say to a well-meaning but domineering parent or a just plain domineering one, "Wait a minute! I am too an artist!" The dreaded response may come back, "How do you know?" And, of course, the fledgling artist does not *know*. There is just this dream, this feeling, this urge, this desire. There is seldom any real proof, but the dream lives on.

As a rule of thumb, shadow artists judge themselves harshly, beating themselves for years over the fact that they have not acted on their dreams. This cruelty only reinforces their status as shadow artists. Remember, it takes nurturing to make an artist. Shadow artists did not receive sufficient nurturing. They blame themselves for not acting fearlessly anyhow.

In a twisted version of Darwinian determinism, we tell ourselves that real artists can survive the most hostile environments and yet find their true calling like homing pigeons. That's hogwash. Many real artists bear children too early or have too many, are too poor or too far removed culturally or monetarily from artistic opportunity to become the artists they really are. These artists, shadow artists through no fault of their own, hear the distant piping of the dream but are unable to make their way through the cultural maze to find it.

For all shadow artists, life may be a discontented experience, filled with a sense of missed purpose and unfulfilled

We have been taught to believe that negative equals realistic and positive equals unrealistic.

SUSAN JEFFERS

Do not weep; do not wax indignant. Understand.

BARUCH SPINOZA

promise. They want to write. They want to paint. They want to act, make music, dance . . . but they are afraid to take themselves seriously.

In order to move from the realm of shadows into the light of creativity, shadow artists must learn to take themselves seriously. With gentle, deliberate effort, they must nurture their artist child. Creativity is play, but for shadow artists, learning to allow themselves to play is hard work.

Protecting the Artist Child Within

Remember, your artist is a child. Find and protect that child. Learning to let yourself create is like learning to walk. The artist child must begin by crawling. Baby steps will follow and there will be falls—yecchy first paintings, beginning films that look like unedited home movies, first poems that would shame a greeting card. Typically, the recovering shadow artist will use these early efforts to discourage continued exploration.

Judging your early artistic efforts is artist abuse. This happens in any number of ways: beginning work is measured against the masterworks of other artists; beginning work is exposed to premature criticism, shown to overly critical friends. In short, the fledgling artist behaves with well-practiced masochism. Masochism is an art form long ago mastered, perfected during the years of self-reproach; this habit is the self-hating bludgeon with which a shadow artist can beat himself right back into the shadows.

In recovering from our creative blocks, it is necessary to go gently and slowly. What we are after here is the healing of old wounds—not the creation of new ones. No high jumping, please! Mistakes are necessary! Stumbles are normal. These are baby steps. Progress, not perfection, is what we should be asking of ourselves.

Too far, too fast, and we can undo ourselves. Creative recovery is like marathon training. We want to log ten slow miles for every one fast mile. This can go against the ego's grain. We want to be great—immediately great—but that is not how recovery works. It is an awkward, tentative, even

To live a creative life, we must lose our fear of being wrong.

JOSEPH CHILTON
PEARCE

When you are feeling depreciated, angry or drained, it is a sign that other people are not open to your energy.

SANAYA ROMAN

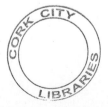

embarrassing process. There will be many times when we won't look good—to ourselves or anyone else. We need to stop demanding that we do. It is impossible to get better and look good at the same time.

Remember that in order to recover as an artist, you must be willing to be a bad artist. Give yourself permission to be a beginner. By being willing to be a bad artist, you have a chance to *be* an artist, and perhaps, over time, a very good one.

When I make this point in teaching, I am met by instant, defensive hostility: "But do you know how old I will be by the time I learn to really play the piano/act/paint/write a decent play?"

Yes . . . the same age you will be if you don't.

So let's start.

YOUR ENEMY WITHIN: CORE NEGATIVE BELIEFS

Most of the time when we are blocked in an area of our life, it is because we feel safer that way. We may not be happy, but at least we know what we are—unhappy. Much fear of our own creativity is the fear of the unknown.

If I am fully creative, what will it mean? What will happen to me and to others? We have some pretty awful notions about what *could* happen. So, rather than find out, we decide to stay blocked. This is seldom a conscious decision. It is more often an unconscious response to internalized negative beliefs. In this week, we will work at uncovering our negative beliefs and discarding them.

Here is a list of commonly held negative beliefs:
I can't be a successful, prolific, creative artist because:

1. Everyone will hate me.

2. I will hurt my friends and family.

3. I will go crazy.

4. I will abandon my friends and family.

5. I can't spell.

Painting is an attempt to come to terms with life. There are as many solutions as there are human beings.

GEORGE TOOKER

6. I don't have good enough ideas.

7. It will upset my mother and/or father.

8. I will have to be alone.

9. I will find out I am gay (if straight).

10. I will be struck straight (if gay).

11. I will do bad work and not know it and look like a fool.

12. I will feel too angry.

13. I will never have any real money.

14. I will get self-destructive and drink, drug, or sex myself to death.

15. I will get cancer, AIDS—or a heart attack or the plague.

16. My lover will leave me.

17. I will die.

18. I will feel bad because I don't deserve to be successful.

19. I will have only one good piece of work in me.

20. It's too late. If I haven't become a fully functioning artist yet, I never will.

None of these core negatives need be true. They come to us from our parents, our religion, our culture, and our fearful friends. Each one of these beliefs reflects notions we have about what it means to be an artist.

Once we have cleared away the most sweeping cultural negatives, we may find we are still stubbornly left with core negatives we have acquired from our families, teachers, and friends. These are often more subtle—but equally undermining if not confronted. Our business here is confronting them.

Negative beliefs are exactly that: beliefs, not facts. The world was never flat, although everyone believed it was. You are not dumb, crazy, egomaniacal, grandiose, or silly just because you falsely believe yourself to be.

What you are is scared. Core negatives keep you scared.

The bottom line is that core negatives—personal and cultural—always go for your jugular. They attack your sexuality, your lovability, your intelligence—whatever vulnerability they can latch on to.

Some core negatives beliefs and their positive alternatives are listed below.

NEGATIVE BELIEFS	POSITIVE ALTERNATIVES
Artists are:	Artists can be:
drunk	sober
crazy	sane
broke	solvent
irresponsible	responsible
loners	user-friendly
promiscuous	faithful
doomed	saved
unhappy	happy
born, not made	discovered and recovered

For example, in a female artist, the artists-are-promiscuous cliché may have in its place a personal negative: "No man will ever love you if you are an artist. Artists are either celibate or gay." This negative, picked up from a mother or teacher and unarticulated by the young artist, can constitute grounds for a powerful block.

Similarly, a young male artist may have the personal negative "Male artists are either gay or impotent." This notion, picked up from a teacher or from reading too much about Fitzgerald and Hemingway, may again create a block. Who wants to be sexually dysfunctional?

A gay artist may have yet anther spin on the ball: "Only heterosexual art is really acceptable, so why make my art if I have to either disguise it or come out of the closet whether I want to or not?"

Stripped to their essence, our multiple negative beliefs reveal a central negative belief: we must trade one good, beloved dream for another. In other words, if being an artist seems too good to be true to you, you will devise a price tag for it that strikes you as unpayable. Hence, you remain blocked.

Most blocked creatives carry unacknowledged either/or reasoning that stands between them and their work. To become unblocked we must recognize our either/or thinking. "I can either be romantically happy *or* an artist." "I can either be financially successful *or* an artist." It is possible, quite possible, to be both an artist and romantically fulfilled. It is quite possible to be an artist and financially successful.

Your block doesn't want you to see that. Its whole plan of attack is to make you irrationally afraid of some dire outcome you are too embarrassed to even mention. You know rationally that writing or painting shouldn't be put off because of your silly fear, but because it is a silly fear, you don't air it and the block stays intact. In this way, "You're a bad speller" successfully overrides all computer spelling programs. You *know* it's dumb to worry about spelling . . . so you don't mention it. And since you don't, it continues to block you from finding a solution. (Spelling fear is a remarkably common block.)

In the next part of this week, we will excavate your unconscious beliefs by using some logic-brain/artist-brain learning tricks. These may strike you as hokey and unproductive. Again, that's resistance. If internalized negativity is the enemy within, what follows is some very effective weaponry. Try it before discarding it out of hand.

I cannot believe that the inscrutable universe turns on an axis of suffering; surely the strange beauty of the world must somewhere rest on pure joy!

LOUISE BOGAN

YOUR ALLY WITHIN: AFFIRMATIVE WEAPONS

As blocked creatives, we often sit on the sidelines critiquing those in the game. "He's not so talented," we may say of a currently hot artist. And we may be right about that. All too often, it is audacity and not talent that moves an artist to center stage. As blocked creatives, we tend to regard these bogus spotlight grabbers with animosity. We may be able to defer to true genius, but if it's merely a genius for self-promotion we're witnessing, our resentment runs high. This is not just jealousy.

It is a stalling technique that reinforces our staying stuck. We make speeches to ourselves and other willing victims: "I could do that better, if only . . ."

You could do it better if only you would let yourself do it!

Affirmations will help you allow yourself to do it. An affirmation is a positive statement of (positive) belief, and if we can become one-tenth as good at positive self-talk as we are at negative self-talk, we will notice an enormous change.

Affirmations help achieve a sense of safety and hope. When we first start working with affirmations, they may feel dumb. Hokey. Embarrassing. Isn't this interesting? We can easily, and without embarrassment, bludgeon ourselves with negative affirmations: "I'm not gifted enough/not clever enough/not original enough/not young enough . . ." But saying nice things about ourselves is notoriously hard to do. It feels pretty awful at first. Try these and see if they don't sound hopelessly syrupy: "I deserve love." "I deserve fair pay." "I deserve a rewarding creative life." "I am a brilliant and successful artist." "I have rich creative talents." "I am competent and confident in my creative work."

Did your Censor perk its nasty little ears up? Censors loathe anything that sounds like real self-worth. They immediately start up with the imposter routine: "Who do you think you are?" It's as though our entire collective unconscious sat up late nights watching Walt Disney's *One Hundred and One Dalmatians* and practicing Cruella DeVille's delivery for scathing indictments.

Just try picking an affirmation. For example "I, _____ (your name), am a brilliant and prolific potter [painter, poet, or whatever you are]." Write that ten times in a row. While you are busy doing that, something very interesting will happen. Your Censor will start to object. "Hey, wait a minute. You can't say all that positive stuff around me." Objections will start to pop up like burnt toast. These are your *blurts*.

Listen to the objections. Look at the ugly, stumpy little blurts. "Brilliant and prolific . . . sure you are. . . . Since when? . . . Can't spell. . . . You call writer's block prolific? . . . You're just kidding yourself . . . an idiot . . . gran-

Affirmations are like prescriptions for certain aspects of yourself you want to change.

JERRY FRANKHAUSER

diose. . . . Who are you kidding? . . . Who do you think you
are?" and so on.

You will be amazed at the rotten things your subconscious
will blurt out. Write them down. These blurts flag your personal negative core beliefs. They hold the key to your freedom
in their ugly little claws. Make a list of your personal blurts.

It's time to do a little detective work. Where do your blurts
come from? Mom? Dad? Teachers? Using your list of blurts,
scan your past for possible sources. At least some of them will
spring violently to mind. One effective way to locate the
sources is to time-travel. Break your life into five-year increments, and list by name your major influences in each time
block.

Paul had *always* wanted to be a writer. And yet, after a brief
flurry of college creativity, he stopped showing his writing to
anyone. Instead of the short stories he dreamed of, he kept
journal after journal, each following the last into a dark drawer
far from prying eyes. Why he did this was a mystery to him
until he tried working with affirmations and blurts.

When Paul began writing his affirmations, he was immediately shaken by an almost volcanic blast of disparagement.

He wrote, "I, Paul, am a brilliant and prolific writer."
From deep in his unconscious there erupted a spewing torrent
of self-abuse and self-doubt. It was numbingly specific and
somehow *familiar:* "You're just kidding yourself, a fool, no real
talent, a pretender, a dilettante, a joke . . ."

Where did this core belief come from? Who could have
said this to him? When? Paul went time-traveling to look for
the villain. He located him with great embarrassment. Yes,
there was a villain, and an incident he had been too ashamed to
share and air. A malevolent early teacher had first praised his
work and then set about a sexual seduction. Fearful that he had
somehow invited the man's attention, ashamed lest the work
really be rotten too, Paul buried the incident in his unconscious, where it festered. No wonder secondary motives were
always a fear when someone praised him. No surprise he felt
that someone could praise work and not mean it.

Boiled down to its essentials, Paul's core negative belief

*The meeting of two personalities
is like the contact of two chemical
substances: if there is any reaction, both are transformed.*

C. G. JUNG

was that he was only kidding himself that he could write. This belief had dominated his thinking for a decade. Whenever people complimented him on his work, he was deeply suspicious of them and their motives. He had all but dropped friends once they had expressed interest in his talents; he had certainly stopped trusting them. When his girlfriend, Mimi, expressed interest in his talents, he even stopped trusting her.

Once Paul brought this monster up from the depths, he could begin to work with it. "I, Paul, have a real talent. I, Paul, trust and enjoy positive feedback. I, Paul, have a real talent. . . ." Although such positive affirmations felt very uncomfortable at first, they rapidly allowed Paul the freedom to participate in the first public reading of his work. When he was widely praised, he was able to accept the good response without discounting it.

CREATIVE AFFIRMATIONS

1. I am a channel for God's creativity, and my work comes to good.

2. My dreams come from God and God has the power to accomplish them.

3. As I create and listen, I will be led.

4. Creativity is the creator's will for me.

5. My creativity heals myself and others.

6. I am allowed to nurture my artist.

7. Through the use of a few simple tools, my creativity will flourish.

8. Through the use of my creativity, I serve God.

9. My creativity always leads me to truth and love.

Turn now to your own list of blurts. They are very important to your recovery. Each of them has held you in bondage. Each of them must be dissolved. For example, a blurt that runs, "I, Fred, am untalented and phony" might be converted to the affirmation "I, Fred, am genuinely talented."

Use your affirmations after your morning pages.
Also use any of the creative affirmations listed.

An affirmation is a strong, positive statement that something is already so.

SHAKTI GAWAIN

TASKS ✉

1. Every morning, set your clock one-half hour early; get up and write three pages of longhand, stream-of-consciousness morning writing. Do not reread these

10. My creativity leads me to forgiveness and self-forgiveness.

11. There is a divine plan of goodness for me.

12. There is a divine plan of goodness for my work.

13. As I listen to the creator within, I am led.

14. As I listen to my creativity I am led to my creator.

15. I am willing to create.

16. I am willing to learn to let myself create.

17. I am willing to let God create through me.

18. I am willing to be of service through my creativity.

19. I am willing to experience my creative energy.

20. I am willing to use my creative talents.

Go confidently in the direction of your dreams! Live the life you've imagined. As you simplify your life, the laws of the universe will be simpler.

HENRY DAVID THOREAU

Make your own recovery the first priority in your life.

ROBIN NORWOOD

pages or allow anyone else to read them. Ideally, stick these pages in a large manila envelope, or hide them somewhere. Welcome to the morning pages. They will change you.

This week, please be sure to work with your affirmations of choice and your blurts at the end of each day's morning pages. Convert all blurts into positive affirmations.

2. Take yourself on an artist date. You will do this every week for the duration of the course. A sample artist date: take five dollars and go to your local five-and-dime. Buy silly things like gold stick-'em stars, tiny dinosaurs, some postcards, sparkly sequins, glue, a kid's scissors, crayons. You might give yourself a gold star on your envelope each day you write. Just for fun.

3. Time Travel: List three old enemies of your creative self-worth. Please be as specific as possible in doing this exercise. Your historic monsters are the building blocks of your core negative beliefs. (Yes, rotten Sister Ann Rita from fifth grade does count, and the rotten thing she said to you does matter. Put her in.) This is your monster hall of fame. More monsters will come to you as you work through your recovery. It is always necessary to acknowledge creative injuries and grieve them. Otherwise, they become creative scar tissue and block your growth.

4. Time Travel: Select and write out one horror story from your monster hall of fame. You do not need to write long or much, but do jot down whatever details come back to you—the room you were in, the way people looked at you, the way you felt, what your parent said or didn't say when you told about it. Include whatever rankles you about the incident: "And then I remember she gave me this real fakey smile and patted my head. . . ."

You may find it cathartic to draw a sketch of your old monster or to clip out an image that evokes the incident for you. Cartoon trashing your monster, or at least draw a nice red *X* through it.

5. Write a letter to the editor in your defense. Mail it to yourself. It is great fun to write this letter in the voice of your wounded artist child: "To whom it may concern: Sister Ann Rita is a jerk and has pig eyes and I can too spell!"

Every time we say Let there be! in any form, something happens.

STELLA TERRILL MANN

6. Time Travel: List three old champions of your creative self-worth. This is your hall of champions, those who wish you and your creativity well. Be specific. Every encouraging word counts. Even if you disbelieve a compliment, record it. It may well be true.

   If you are stuck for compliments, go back through your time-travel log and look for positive memories. When, where, and why did you feel good about yourself? Who gave you affirmation?

   Additionally, you may wish to write the compliment out and decorate it. Post it near where you do your morning pages or on the dashboard of your car. I put mine on the chassis of my computer to cheer me as I write.

7. Time Travel: Select and write out one happy piece of encouragement. Write a thank-you letter. Mail it to yourself or to the long-lost mentor.

8. Imaginary Lives: If you had five other lives to lead, what would you do in each of them? I would be a pilot, a cowhand, a physicist, a psychic, a monk. You might be a scuba diver, a cop, a writer of children's books, a football player, a belly dancer, a painter, a performance artist, a history teacher, a healer, a coach, a scientist, a doctor, a Peace Corps worker, a psychologist, a fisherman, a minister, an auto mechanic, a carpenter, a sculptor, a lawyer, a painter, a computer hacker, a soap-opera star, a country singer, a rock-and-roll drummer. Whatever occurs to you, jot it down. Do not overthink this exercise.

   The point of these lives is to have fun in them—

Undoubtedly, we become what we envisage.

CLAUDE M. BRISTOL

more fun than you might be having in this one. Look over your list and select one. Then do it this week. For instance, if you put down *country singer*, can you pick a guitar? If you dream of being a cowhand, what about some horseback riding?

9. In working with affirmations and blurts, very often injuries and monsters swim back to us. Add these to your list as they occur to you. Work with each blurt individually. Turn each negative into an affirmative positive.

10. Take your artist for a walk, the two of you. A brisk twenty-minute walk can dramatically alter consciousness.

CHECK-IN ✐

You will do check-ins every week. If you are running your creative week Sunday to Sunday, do your check-ins each Saturday. Remember that this recovery is *yours*. What you think is important, and it will become increasingly interesting to you as you progress. You may want to do check-ins in your morning-pages notebook. It's best to answer by hand and allow about twenty minutes to respond. The purpose of check-ins is to give you a journal of your creative journey. It is my hope that you will later share the tools with others and in doing so find your own notes invaluable: "Yes, I was mad in week four. I loved week five. . . ."

1. How many days this week did you do your morning pages? Seven out of seven, we always hope. How was the experience for you?

2. Did you do your artist date this week? Yes, of course, we always hope. And yet artist dates can be remarkably difficult to allow yourself. What did you do? How did it feel?

3. Were there any other issues this week that you consider significant for your recovery? Describe them.

Recovering a Sense of Identity

This week addresses self-definition as a major component of creative recovery. You may find yourself drawing new bound-aries and staking out new territories as your personal needs, desires, and interests announce themselves. The essays and tools are aimed at moving you into your per-sonal identity, a self-defined you.

GOING SANE

TRUSTING OUR CREATIVITY IS new behavior for many of us. It may feel quite threatening initially, not only to us but also to our intimates. We may feel—and look—erratic. This errati-cism is a normal part of getting unstuck, pulling free from the muck that has blocked us. It is important to remember that at first flush, going *sane* feels just like going crazy.

There is a recognizable ebb and flow to the process of re-covering our creative selves. As we gain strength, so will some of the attacks of self-doubt. This is normal, and we can deal with these stronger attacks when we see them as symptoms of recovery.

Common self-attacks are: "Okay, so I did okay this week but it's just a temporary thing. . . . Okay, so I got the morning pages done. I probably did them wrong. . . . Okay, so now I need to plan something big and do it *right away!* . . . Who am I kidding? I'll never recover, not right away . . . not ever. . . ."

These attacks are groundless, but very convincing to our-selves. Buying into them enables us to remain stuck and

All sanity depends on this: that it should be a delight to feel heat strike the skin, a delight to stand upright, knowing the bones are moving easily under the flesh.

DORIS LESSING

Snipers are people who undermine your efforts to break unhealthy relationship patterns.

JODY HAYES

victimized. Just as a recovering alcoholic must avoid the first drink, the recovering artist must avoid taking the first *think*. For us, that think is really self-doubt: "I don't *think* this is any good. . . ."

These attacks can come from either internal or external sources. We can neutralize them once we recognize them as a sort of creative virus. Affirmations are a powerful antidote for self-hate, which commonly appears under the mask of self-doubt.

Early in our creative recovery, self-doubt can lure us into self-sabotage. A common form for this sabotage is showing someone our morning pages. Remember, the morning pages are private and are not intended for the scrutiny of well-meaning friends. One newly unblocked writer showed his morning pages to a writer friend who was still blocked. When she critiqued them, he blocked again.

Do not let your self-doubt turn into self-sabotage.

POISONOUS PLAYMATES

Creativity flourishes when we have a sense of safety and self-acceptance. Your artist, like a small child, is happiest when feeling a sense of security. As our artist's protective parent, we must learn to place our artist with safe companions. Toxic playmates can capsize our artist's growth.

Not surprisingly, the most poisonous playmates for us as recovering creatives are people whose creativity is still blocked. Our recovery threatens them.

As long as we were blocked, we often felt that it was arrogance and self-will to speak of ourselves as creative artists. The truth is that it was self-will to refuse to acknowledge our creativity. Of course, this refusal had its payoffs.

We could wonder and worry abut our arrogance instead of being humble enough to ask help to move through our fear. We could fantasize about art instead of doing the work. By not asking the Great Creator's help with our creativity, and by not seeing the Great Creator's hand in our creativity, we could proceed to righteously ignore our creativity and never have to take the risks of fulfilling it. Your blocked friends may still be in-dulging in all these comforting self-delusions.

If they are having trouble with your recovery, they are still getting a payoff from remaining blocked. Perhaps they still get an anorectic high from the martyrdom of being blocked or they still collect sympathy and wallow in self-pity. Perhaps they still feel smug thinking about how much more creative they *could* be than those who are out there doing it. These are toxic behaviors for you now.

Do not expect your blocked friends to applaud your recov-ery. That's like expecting your best friends from the bar to cel-ebrate your sobriety. How can they when their own drinking is something they want to hold on to?

Blocked friends may find your recovery disturbing. Your getting unblocked raises the unsettling possibility that they, too, could become unblocked and move into authentic creative risks rather than bench-sitting cynicism. Be alert to subtle sabotage from friends. You cannot afford their well-meaning doubts right now. Their doubts will reactivate your own. Be par-ticularly alert to any suggestion that you have become selfish or different. (These are red-alert words for us. They are at-tempts to leverage us back into our old ways for the sake of someone else's comfort, not our own.)

Blocked creatives are easily manipulated by guilt. Our friends, feeling abandoned by our departure from the ranks of the blocked, may unconsciously try to guilt-trip us into giving up our newly healthy habits. It is very important to understand that the time given to morning pages is time between you and God. You best know your answers. You will be led to new sources of support as you begin to support yourself.

Be very careful to safeguard your newly recovering artist. Often, creativity is blocked by our falling in with other people's plans for us. We want to set aside time for our creative work, but we feel we *should* do something else instead. As blocked creatives, we focus not on our responsibilities to ourselves, but on our responsibilities to others. We tend to think such behavior makes us good people. It doesn't. It makes us frustrated people.

The essential element in nurturing our creativity lies in nurturing ourselves. Through self-nurturance we nurture our

To know what you prefer instead of humbly saying Amen to what the world tells you you ought to prefer, is to have kept your soul alive.

ROBERT LOUIS
STEVENSON

Every time you don't follow your inner guidance, you feel a loss of energy, loss of power, a sense of spiritual deadness.

SHAKTI GAWAIN

inner connection to the Great Creator. Through this connection our creativity will unfold. Paths will appear for us. We need to trust the Great Creator and move out in faith.

Repeat: the Great Creator has gifted us with creativity. Our gift back is our use of it. Do not let friends squander your time.

Be gentle but firm, and hang tough. The best thing you can do for your friends is to be an example through your own recovery. Do not let their fears and second thoughts derail you.

Soon enough, the techniques you learn will enable you to teach others. Soon enough, you will be a bridge that will allow others to cross over from self-doubt into self-expression. For right now, protect your artist by refusing to show your morning pages to interested bystanders or to share your artist date with friends. Draw a sacred circle around your recovery. Give yourself the gift of faith. Trust that you are on the right track. You are.

As your recovery progresses, you will come to experience a more comfortable faith in your creator and your creator within. You will learn that it is actually easier to write than not write, paint than not paint, and so forth. You will learn to enjoy the process of being a creative channel and to surrender your need to control the result. You will discover the joy of *practicing* your creativity. The process, not the product, will become your focus.

You own healing is the greatest message of hope for others.

CRAZYMAKERS

A related thing creatives do to avoid being creative is to involve themselves with *crazymakers*. Crazymakers are those personalities that create storm centers. They are often charismatic, frequently charming, highly inventive, and powerfully persuasive. And, for the creative person in their vicinity, they are enormously destructive. You know the type: charismatic but out of control, long on problems and short on solutions.

Crazymakers are the kind of people who can take over your whole life. To fixer-uppers, they are irresistible: so much to change, so many distractions. . . .

If you are involved with a crazymaker, you probably know

it already, and you certainly recognize the thumbnail description in the paragraph above. Crazymakers like drama. If they can swing it, they are the star. Everyone around them functions as supporting cast, picking up their cues, their entrances and exits, from the crazymaker's (crazy) whims.

Some of the most profoundly destructive crazymakers I have ever encountered are themselves famous artists. They are the kind of artists that give the rest of us bad names. Often larger than life, they acquire that status by feeding on the life energies of those around them. For this reason, many of the most crazy artists in America are found surrounded by a cadre of supporters as talented as they are but determined to subvert their own talent in the service of the Crazymaking King.

Learn to get in touch with the silence within yourself and know that everything in this life has a purpose.

ELISABETH
KÜBLER-ROSS

I am thinking of a movie set I visited several years ago. The filmmaker was one of the giants of American cinema. His stature was unmistakable, and so was his identity as a crazymaker. Given that all filmmaking is demanding, his sets are far more so: longer hours; long bouts of paranoia; intrigue and internecine politics. Amid rumors that the set was bugged, this Crazymaker King addressed his actors over a loudspeaker system while he, like the Wizard of Oz, secreted himself away in a large and luxuriously equipped trailer cave.

Over the past two decades, I have watched many directors at work. I was married to a profoundly gifted director, and I have directed a feature myself. I have often remarked how closely a film crew resembles an extended family. In the case of this Crazymaker King, the crew resembled nothing so much as an alcoholic family: the alcoholic drinker (thinker) surrounded by his tiptoeing enablers, all pretending that his outsized ego and its concomitant demands were normal.

On that crazymaker's set, the production lurched off schedule and over budget from king baby's unreasonable demands. A film crew is essentially a crew of experts, and to watch these estimable experts become disheartened was a strong lesson for me in the poisonous power of crazymaking. Brilliant set designers, costume designers, sound engineers—not to mention actors—became increasingly injured as the production ran its devastating course. It was against the crazymaking director's personal dramas that they struggled to create the drama that was meant to go onscreen. Like all good movie people, this crew was willing to work long hours for good work. What discouraged them was working those hours in the service of ego instead of art.

The crazymaking dynamic is grounded in power, and so any group of people can function as an energy system to be exploited and drained. Crazymakers can be found in almost any setting, in almost any art form. Fame may help to create them, but since they feed on power, any power source will do. Although quite frequently crazymakers are found among the rich and famous, they are common even among commoners. Right in the nuclear family (there's a reason we use that word), a resident crazymaker may often be found pitting family member against family member, undercutting anyone's agenda but his or her own.

I am thinking now of a destructive matriarch of my acquaintance. The titular head of a large and talented clan, she has devoted her extensive energies to destroying the creativity of her children. Always choosing critical moments for her sabotage, she plants her bombs to explode just as her children approach success.

The daughter struggling to finish a belated college degree finds herself saddled with a suddent drama the night before her final exam. The son with a critical job interview is gifted with a visitation just when he needs to focus the most.

"Do you know what the neighbors are saying about you?" the crazymaker will often ask. (And the beleaguered student mother will hear a horrific round of gossip that leaves her battered, facing her exam week beset by feelings of "What's the use?")

"Do you realize you're ruining your own marriage with this possible new job?" (And the son's hopeful career move is ashes before it begins.)

Whether they appear as your overbearing mother, your manic boss, your needy friend, or your stubborn spouse, the crazymakers in your life share certain destructive patterns that make them poisonous for any sustained creative work.

Crazymakers break deals and destroy schedules. They show up two days early for your wedding and expect to be waited on hand and foot. They rent a vacation cabin larger and more expensive than the one agreed upon, and then they expect you to foot the bill.

Crazymakers expect special treatment. They suffer a wide panoply of mysterious ailments that require care and attention whenever you have a deadline looming—or anything else that draws your attention from the crazymaker's demands. The crazymaker cooks her own special meal in a house full of hungry children—and does nothing to feed the kids. The crazymaker is too upset to drive right after he has vented enormous verbal abuse on the heads of those around him. "I am afraid Daddy will have a heart attack," the victim starts thinking, instead of, "How do I get this monster out of my house?"

Crazymakers discount your reality. No matter how important your deadline or how critical your work trajectory at the moment, crazymakers will violate your needs. They may act as though they hear your boundaries and will respect them, but in practice *act* is the operative word. Crazymakers are the people who call you at midnight or 6:00 A.M. saying, "I know you asked me not to call you at this time, but . . ." Crazymakers are the people who drop by unexpectedly to borrow something you can't find or don't want to lend them. Even better, they call and ask you to locate something they need, then fail to pick it up. "I know you're on a deadline," they say, "but this will only take a minute." Your minute.

Crazymakers spend your time and money. If they borrow your car, they return it late, with an empty tank. Their travel arrangements always cost you time or money. They demand to be met in the middle of your workday at an airport miles from town. "I didn't bring taxi money," they say when confronted with, "But I'm working."

Crazymakers triangulate those they deal with. Because crazymakers thrive on energy (your energy), they set people against one another in order to maintain their own power position dead center. (That's where they can feed most directly on the negative energies they stir up.) "So-and-so was telling me you didn't get to work on time today," a crazymaker may relay. You

What I am actually saying is that we need to be willing to let our intuition guide us, and then be willing to follow that guidance directly and fearlessly.

SHAKTI GAWAIN

obligingly get mad at so-and-so and miss the fact that the crazymaker has used hearsay to set you off kilter emotionally.

Crazymakers are expert blamers. Nothing that goes wrong is ever their fault, and to hear them tell it, the fault is usually yours. "If you hadn't cashed that child-support check it would never have bounced," one crazymaking ex-husband told his struggling-for-serenity former spouse.

Crazymakers create dramas—but seldom where they belong. Crazymakers are often blocked creatives themselves. Afraid to effectively tap their own creativity, they are loath to allow that same creativity in others. It makes them jealous. It makes them threatened. It makes them dramatic—at your expense. Devoted to their own agendas, crazymakers impose these agendas on others. In dealing with a crazymaker, you are dealing always with the famous issue of figure and ground. In other words, whatever matters to you becomes trivialized into mere backdrop for the crazymaker's personal plight. "Do you think he/she loves me?" they call you to ask when you are trying to pass the bar exam or get your husband home from the hospital.

Crazymakers hate schedules—except their own. In the hands of a crazymaker, time is a primary tool for abuse. If you claim a certain block of time as your own, your crazymaker will find a way to fight you for that time, to mysteriously need things (meaning you) just when you need to be alone and focused on the task at hand. "I stayed up until three last night. I can't drive the kids to school," the crazymaker will spring on you the morning you yourself must leave early for a business breakfast with your boss.

Crazymakers hate order. Chaos serves their purposes. When you begin to establish a place that serves you and your creativity, your crazymaker will abruptly invade that space with projects of his/her own. "What are all these papers, all this laundry on top of my work table?" you ask. "I decided to sort my college papers . . . to start looking for the matches for my socks . . ."

Slow down and enjoy life. It's not only the scenery you miss by going too fast—you also miss the sense of where you are going and why.

EDDIE CANTOR

Crazymakers deny that they are crazymakers. They go for the jugular. "I am not what's making you crazy," your crazymaker may say when you point out a broken promise or a piece of sabotage. "It's just that we have such a rotten sex life."

If crazymakers are that destructive, what are we doing involved with them? The answer, to be brief but brutal, is that we're that crazy ourselves and we are that self-destructive.

Really?

Yes. As blocked creatives, we are willing to go to almost any lengths to remain blocked. As frightening and abusive as life with a crazymaker is, we find it far less threatening than the challenge of a creative life of our own. What would happen then? What would we be like? Very often, we fear that if we let ourselves be creative, we will become crazymakers ourselves and abuse those around us. Using this fear as our excuse, we continue to allow others to abuse us.

If you are involved now with a crazymaker, it is very important that you admit this fact. Admit that you are being used—and admit that you are using your own abuser. Your crazymaker is a block you chose yourself, to deter you from your own trajectory. As much as you are being exploited by your crazymaker, you, too, are using that person to block your creative flow.

If you are involved in a tortured tango with a crazymaker, stop dancing to his/her tune. Pick up a book on codependency or get yourself to a twelve-step program for relationship addiction. (Al-Anon and Sex and Love Addicts Anonymous are two excellent programs for stopping the crazymaker's dance.)

The next time you catch yourself saying or thinking, "He/she is driving me crazy!" ask yourself what creative work you are trying to block by your involvement.

Whatever God's dream about man may be, it seems certain it cannot come true unless man cooperates.

STELLA TERRILL MANN

SKEPTICISM

Now that we have talked about the barrier to recovery others can present, let us take a look at the inner enemy we harbor ourselves. Perhaps the greatest barrier for any of us as we look for an expanded life is our own deeply held skepticism. This might be called *the secret doubt*. It does not seem to matter whether we are officially believers or agnostics. We have our doubts about all of this creator/creativity stuff, and those doubts are very powerful. Unless we air them, they can sabotage us. Many times, in trying to be good sports we stuff our feelings of doubt. We need to stop doing that and explore them instead.

Boiled down to their essentials, the doubts go something like this: "Okay, so I started writing the morning pages and I seem more awake and alert in my life. So what? It's just a coincidence. . . . Okay, so I have started filling the well and taking my artist on a date and I do notice I am cheering up a little. So what? It's just coincidental. . . . Okay, so now I am beginning to notice that the more I let myself explore the possibility of there being some power for good, the more I notice lucky coincidence turning up in my life. So what? I can't believe I am really being led. That's just too weird. . . ."

The reason we think it's weird to imagine an unseen helping hand is that we still doubt that it's okay for us to be creative. With this attitude firmly entrenched, we not only look all gift horses in the mouth but also swat them on the rump to get them out of our lives as fast as possible.

When Mike began his creative recovery, he let himself admit that he wanted to make films. Two weeks later, through a series of "coincidences," he found himself in film school with his company paying for it. Did he relax and enjoy this? No. He told himself that film school was distracting him from his real job of finding another job. And so he gave up filmmaking to look for another job.

Two years later, remembering this incident, Mike can shake his head at himself. When the universe gave him what he wanted, he gave the gift right back. Eventually, he did let himself learn filmmaking, but he made it a lot harder on himself than the universe may have intended.

One of the things most worth noting in a creative recovery is our reluctance to take seriously the possibility that the universe just might be cooperating with our new and expanded

To believe in God or in a guiding force because someone tells you to is the height of stupidity. We are given senses to receive our information with. With our own eyes we see, and with our skin we feel. With our intelligence, it is intended that we understand. But each person must puzzle it out for himself or herself.

SOPHY BURNHAM

plans. We've gotten brave enough to try recovery, but we don't want the universe to really pay attention. We still feel too much like frauds to handle some success. When it comes, we want to go.

Of course we do! Any little bit of experimenting in self-nurturance is very frightening for most of us. When our little experiment provokes the universe to open a door or two, we start shying away. "Hey! You! Whatever you are! Not so fast!"

I like to think of the mind as a room. In that room, we keep all of our usual ideas about life, God, what's possible and what's not. The room has a door. That door is ever so slightly ajar, and outside we can see a great deal of dazzling light. Out there in the dazzling light are a lot of new ideas that we consider too far-out for us, and so we keep them out there. The ideas we are comfortable with are in the room with us. The other ideas are out, and we keep them out.

In our ordinary, prerecovery life, when we would hear something weird or threatening, we'd just grab the doorknob and pull the door shut. Fast.

Inner work triggering outer change? Ridiculous! (Slam the door.) God bothering to help my *own* creative recovery? (Slam.) Synchronicity supporting my artist with serendipitous coincidences? (Slam, slam, slam.)

Now that we are in creative recovery, there is another approach we need to try. To do this, we gently set aside our skepticism—for later use, if we need it—and when a weird idea or coincidence whizzes by, we gently nudge the door a little further open.

Setting skepticism aside, even briefly, can make for very interesting explorations. In creative recovery, it is not necessary that we change any of our beliefs. It is necessary that we examine them.

More than anything else, creative recovery is an exercise in open-mindedness. Again, picture your mind as that room with the door slightly ajar. Nudging the door open a bit more is what makes for open-mindedness. Begin, this week, to consciously practice opening your mind.

Think of yourself as an incandescent power, illuminated and perhaps forever talked to by God and his messengers.

BRENDA UELAND

No matter how slow the film, Spirit always stands still long enough for the photographer It has chosen.

MINOR WHITE

ATTENTION

Develop interest in life as you see it; in people, things, literature, music—the world is so rich, simply throbbing with rich treasures, beautiful souls and interesting people. Forget yourself.

HENRY MILLER

Very often, a creative block manifests itself as an addiction to fantasy. Rather than working or living the now, we spin our wheels and indulge in daydreams of could have, would have, should have. One of the great misconceptions about the artistic life is that it entails great swathes of aimlessness. The truth is that a creative life involves great swathes of attention. Attention is a way to connect and survive.

"Flora and fauna reports," I used to call the long, winding letters from my grandmother. "The forsythia is starting and this morning I saw my first robin. . . . The roses are holding even in this heat. . . . The sumac has turned and that little maple down by the mailbox. . . . My Christmas cactus is getting ready. . . ."

I followed my grandmother's life like a long home movie: a shot of this and a shot of that, spliced together with no pattern that I could ever see. "Dad's cough is getting worse. . . . The little Shetland looks like she'll drop her foal early. . . . Joanne is back in the hospital at Anna. . . . We named the new boxer Trixie and she likes to sleep in my cactus bed—can you imagine?"

I could imagine. Her letters made that easy. Life through grandma's eyes was a series of small miracles: the wild tiger lilies under the cottonwoods in June; the quick lizard scooting under the gray river rock she admired for its satiny finish. Her letters clocked the seasons of the year and her life. She lived until she was eighty, and the letters came until the very end. When she died, it was as suddenly as her Christmas cactus: here today, gone tomorrow. She left behind her letters and her husband of sixty-two years. Her husband, my grandfather Daddy Howard, an elegant rascal with a gambler's smile and a loser's luck, had made and lost several fortunes, the last of them permanently. He drank them away, gambled them away, tossed them away the way she threw crumbs to her birds. He squandered life's big chances the way she savored the small ones. "That man," my mother would say.

My grandmother lived with that man in tiled Spanish houses, in trailers, in a tiny cabin halfway up a mountain, in a railroad flat, and, finally, in a house made out of ticky-tacky where they all looked just the same. "I don't know how she stands it," my mother would say, furious with my grandfather for some new misadventure. She meant she didn't know why.

The truth is, we all knew how she stood it. She stood it by standing knee-deep in the flow of life and paying close attention.

My grandmother was gone before I learned the lesson her letters were teaching: survival lies in sanity, and sanity lies in paying attention. Yes, her letters said, Dad's cough is getting worse, we have lost the house, there is no money and no work, but the tiger lilies are blooming, the lizard has found that spot of sun, the roses are holding despite the heat.

My grandmother knew what a painful life had taught her: success or failure, the truth of a life really has little to do with its quality. The quality of life is in proportion, always, to the capacity for delight. The capacity for delight is the gift of paying attention.

In a year when a long and rewarding love affair was lurching gracelessly away from the center of her life, the writer May Sarton kept *A Journal of a Solitude*. In it, she records coming home from a particularly painful weekend with her lover. Entering her empty house, "I was stopped by the threshold of my study by a ray on a Korean chrysanthemum, lighting it up like a spotlight, deep red petals and Chinese yellow center. . . . Seeing it was like getting a transfusion of autumn light."

It's no accident that May Sarton uses the word *transfusion*. The loss of her lover was a wound, and in her responses to that chrysanthemum, in the act of paying attention, Sarton's healing began.

The reward for attention is always healing. It may begin as the healing of a particular pain—the lost lover, the sickly child, the shattered dream. But what is healed, finally, is the pain that underlies all pain: the pain that we are all, as Rilke phrases it, "unutterably alone." More than anything else, attention is an act of connection. I learned this the way I have learned most things—quite by accident.

When my first marriage blew apart, I took a lonely house in the Hollywood Hills. My plan was simple. I would weather my loss alone. I would see no one, and no one would see me, until the worst of the pain was over. I would take long, solitary walks, and I would suffer. As it happened, I did take those walks, but they did not go as planned.

Two curves up the road behind my house, I met a gray striped cat. This cat lived in a vivid blue house with a large sheepdog she clearly disliked. I learned all this despite myself in a week's walking. We began to have little visits, that cat and I, and then long talks of all we had in common, lonely women.

Both of us admired an extravagant salmon rose that had wandered across a neighboring fence. Both of us like watching the lavender float of jacaranda blossoms as they shook loose from their moorings. Alice (I heard her called inside one afternoon) would bat at them with her paw.

By the time the jacarandas were done, an unattractive slatted fence had been added to contain the rose garden. By then, I had extended my walks a mile farther up and added to my fellowship other cats, dogs, and children. By the time the salmon rose disappeared behind its fence, I had found a house higher up with a walled Moorish garden and a vitriolic parrot I grew fond of. Colorful, opinionated, highly dramatic, he reminded me of my ex-husband. Pain had become something more valuable: experience.

Writing about attention, I see that I have written a good deal about pain. This is no coincidence. It may be different for others, but pain is what it took to teach me to pay attention. In times of pain, when the future is too terrifying to contemplate and the past too painful to remember, I have learned to pay attention to right now. The precise moment I was in was always the only safe place for me. Each moment, taken alone, was always bearable. In the exact now, we are all, always, all right. Yesterday the marriage may have ended. Tomorrow the cat may die. The phone call from the lover, for all my waiting, may not ever come, but just at the moment, just now, that's all right. I am breathing in and out. Realizing this, I began to notice that each moment was not without its beauty.

The night my mother died, I got the call, took my sweater, and set out up the hill behind my house. A great snowy moon was rising behind the palm trees. Later that night, it floated

The noun of self becomes a verb. This flashpoint of creation in the present moment is where work and play merge.

STEPHEN
NACHMANOVITCH

above the garden, washing the cactus silver. When I think now about my mother's death, I remember that snowy moon.

The poet William Meredith has observed that the worst that can be said of a man is that "he did not pay attention." When I think of my grandmother, I remember her gardening,

The painting has a life of its own. I try to let it come through.

JACKSON POLLOCK

RULES OF THE ROAD

In order to be an artist, I must:

1. Show up at the page. Use the page to rest, to dream, to try.

2. Fill the well by caring for my artist.

3. Set small and gentle goals and meet them.

4. Pray for guidance, courage, and humility.

5. Remember that it is far harder and more painful to be a blocked artist than it is to do the work.

6. Be alert, always, for the presence of the Great Creator leading and helping my artist.

7. Choose companions who encourage me to do the work, not just talk about doing the work or why I am not doing the work.

8. Remember that the Great Creator loves creativity.

9. Remember that it is my job to do the work, not judge the work.

10. Place this sign in my workplace: Great Creator, I will take care of the *quantity.* You take care of the *quality.*

one small, brown breast slipping unexpectedly free from the halter top of the little print dress she made for herself each summer. I remember her pointing down the steep slope from the home she was about to lose, to the cottonwoods in the wash below. "The ponies like them for their shade," she said. "I like them because they go all silvery in their green."

TASKS ✉

1. Affirmative Reading: Every day, morning and night, get quiet and focused and read the Basic Principles to yourself. (See page 3.) Be alert for any attitudinal shifts. Can you see yourself setting aside any skepticism yet?

2. Where does your time go? List your five major activities this week. How much time did you give to each one? Which were what you wanted to do and which were shoulds? How much of your time is spent helping others and ignoring your own desires? Have any of your blocked friends triggered doubts in you?

   Take a sheet of paper. Draw a circle. Inside that circle, place topics you need to protect. Place the names of those you find to be supportive. Outside the circle, place the names of those you must be self-protective around just now. Place this safety map near where you write your morning pages. Use this map to support your autonomy. Add names to the inner and outer spheres as appropriate: "Oh! Derek is somebody I shouldn't talk to about this right now."

3. List twenty things you enjoy doing (rock climbing, roller-skating, baking pies, making soup, making love, making love again, riding a bide, riding a horse, playing catch, shooting baskets, going for a run, reading poetry, and so forth). When was the last time you let yourself do these things? Next to each entry, place a date. Don't be surprised if it's been years for

some of your favorites. That will change. This list is
an excellent resource for artist dates.

4. From the list above, write down two favorite things
    that you've avoided that could be this week's goals.
    These goals can be small: buy one roll of film and
    shoot it. Remember, we are trying to win you some
    autonomy with your time. Look for windows of
    time just for you, and use them in small creative acts.
    Get to the record store at lunch hour, even if only for
    fifteen minutes. Stop looking for big blocks of time
    when you will be free. Find small bits of time in-
    stead.

5. Dip back into Week One and read the affirmations.
    Note which ones cause the most reaction. Often the
    one that sounds the most ridiculous is the most sig-
    nificant. Write three chosen affirmations five times
    each day in your morning pages; be sure to include
    the affirmations you made yourself from your
    blurts.

6. Return to the list of imaginary lives from last week.
    Add five more lives. Again, check to see if you could
    be doing bits and pieces of these lives in the one you
    are living now. If you have listed a dancer's life, do
    you let yourself go dancing? If you have listed a
    monk's life, are you ever allowed to go on a retreat? If
    you are a scuba diver, is there an aquarium shop you
    can visit? A day at the lake you could schedule?

7. Life Pie: Draw a circle. Divide it into six pieces of pie.
    Label one piece *spirituality,* another *exercise,* another
    play, and so on with *work, friends,* and *romance/
    adventure.* Place a dot in each slice at the degree to
    which you are fulfilled in that area (outer rim indi-
    cates great; inner circle, not so great). Connect the
    dots. This will show you where you are lopsided.

    As you begin the course, it is not uncommon for
    your life pie to look like a tarantula. As recovery
    progresses, your tarantula may become a mandala.

Working with this tool, you will notice that there are areas of your life that feel impoverished and on which you spend little or no time. Use the time tidbits you are finding to alter this.

If your spiritual life is minimal, even a five-minute pit stop into a synagogue or cathedral can restore a sense of wonder. Many of us find that five minutes of drum music can put us in touch with our spiritual core. For others, it's a trip to a greenhouse. The point is that even the slightest attention to our impoverished areas can nurture them.

8. Ten Tiny Changes: List ten changes you'd like to make for yourself, from the significant to the small or vice versa ("get new sheets so I have another set, go to China, paint my kitchen, dump my bitchy friend Alice"). Do it this way:

   I would like to _____.

   I would like to _____.

As the morning pages nudge us increasingly into the present, where we pay attention to our current lives, a small shift like a newly painted bathroom can yield a luxuriously large sense of self-care.

9. Select one small item and make it a goal for this week.

10. Now do that item.

I shut my eyes in order to see.

PAUL GAUGUIN

CHECK-IN ✏

1. How many days this week did you do your morning pages? (We're hoping seven, remember.) How was the experience for you? How did the morning pages work for you? Describe them (for example, "They felt so stupid. I'd write all these itty-bitty disconnected things that didn't seem to have anything to do with one another or with anything . . ."). Remem-

ber, if you *are* writing morning pages, they are working for you. What were you surprised to find yourself writing about? Answer this question in full on your check-in page. This will be a weekly self-scan of your moods, not your progress. Don't worry if your pages are whiny and trite. Sometimes that's the very best thing for you.

2. Did you do your artist date this week? Remember that artist dates are a necessary frivolity. What did you do? How did it feel?

3. Were there any other issues this week that you consider significant for your recovery? Describe them.

Recovering a Sense of Power

ANGER

ANGER IS FUEL. We feel it and we want to do something. Hit someone, break something, throw a fit, smash a fist into the wall, tell those bastards. But we are *nice* people, and what we do with our anger is stuff it, deny it, bury it, block it, hide it, lie about it, medicate it, muffle it, ignore it. We do everything but *listen* to it.

Anger is meant to be listened to. Anger is a voice, a shout, a plea, a demand. Anger is meant to be respected. Why? Because anger is a *map*. Anger shows us what our boundaries are. Anger shows us where we want to go. It lets us see where we've been and lets us know when we haven't liked it. Anger points the way, not just the finger. In the recovery of a blocked artist, an-ger is a sign of health.

Anger is meant to be acted upon. It is not meant to be acted out. Anger points the direction. We are meant to use anger as fuel to take the actions we need to move where our anger points us. With a little thought, we can usually translate the message that our anger is sending us.

*I merely took the energy it takes
to pout and wrote some blues.*

DUKE ELLINGTON

"Blast him! I could make a better film than that!" (This anger says: you want to make movies. You need to learn how.)

"I can't believe it! I had this idea for a play three years ago, and she's gone and written it." (This anger says: stop procrastinating. Ideas don't get opening nights. Finished plays do. Start writing.)

"That's my strategy he's using. This is incredible! I've been ripped off! I knew I shoud have pulled that material together and copyrighted it." (This anger says: it's time to take your own ideas seriously enough to treat them well.)

When we feel anger, we are often very angry *that* we feel anger. Damn anger!! It tells us we can't get away with our old life any longer. It tells us that old life is dying. It tells us we are being reborn, and birthing hurts. The hurt makes us angry.

Anger is the firestorm that signals the death of our old life. Anger is the fuel that propels us into our new one. Anger is a tool, not a master. Anger is meant to be tapped into and drawn upon. Used properly, anger is *use-full.*

Sloth, apathy, and despair are the enemy. Anger is not. Anger is our friend. Not a nice friend. Not a gentle friend. But a very, very loyal friend. It will always tell us when we have been betrayed. It will always tell us when we have betrayed ourselves. It will always tell us that it is time to act in our own best interests.

Anger is not the action itself. It is action's invitation.

SYNCHRONICITY

Answered prayers are scary. They imply responsibility. You asked for it. Now that you've got it, what are you going to do? Why else the cautionary phrase "Watch out for what you pray for; you just might get it"? Answered prayers deliver us back to our own hand. This is not comfortable. We find it easier to accept them as examples of synchronicity:

- A woman admits to a buried dream of acting. At dinner the next night, she sits beside a man who teaches beginning actors.

- A writer acknowledges a dream to go to film school. A single exploratory phone call puts him in touch with a professor who knows and admires his work and promises him that the last available slot is now his.

- A woman is thinking about going back to school and opens her mail to find a letter requesting her application from the very school she was thinking about going to.

- A woman wonders how to rent a rare film she has never seen. She finds it at her neighborhood *bookstore* two days later.

- A businessman who has secretly written for years vows to himself to ask a professional writer for a prognosis on his talent. The next night, over a pool table, he meets a writer who becomes his mentor and then collaborator on several successful books.

When a man takes one step toward God, God takes more steps toward that man than there are sands in the worlds of time.

THE WORK OF THE CHARIOT

The universe will reward you for taking risks on its behalf.

SHAKTI GAWAIN

It's my experience that we're much more afraid that there might be a God than we are that there might not be. Incidents like those above happen to us, and yet we dismiss them as sheer coincidence. People talk about how dreadful it would be if there were no God. I think such talk is hooey. Most of us are a lot more comfortable feeling we're not being watched too closely.

If God—by which I do not necessarily mean a single-pointed Christian concept but an all-powerful and all-knowing force—does not exist, well then, we're all off the hook, aren't we? There's no divine retribution, no divine consolation. And if the whole experience stinks—ah well. What did you expect?

That question of expectations interests me. If there is no God, or if that God is disinterested in our puny little affairs, then everything can roll along as always and we can feel quite justified in declaring certain things impossible, other things unfair. If God, or the lack of God, is responsible for the state of the world, then we can easily wax cynical and resign ourselves to apathy. What's the use? Why try changing anything?

This is the use. If there is a responsive creative force that

A discovery is said to be an accident meeting a prepared mind.

ALBERT SZENT-
GYORGYI

Did you ever observe to whom the accidents happen? Chance favors only the prepared mind.

LOUIS PASTEUR

does hear us and act on our behalf, then we may really be able to do some things. The jig, in short, is up: God knows that the sky's the limit. Anyone honest will tell you that possibility is far more frightening than impossibility, that freedom is far more terrifying than any prison. If we do, in fact, have to deal with a force beyond ourselves that involves itself in our lives, then we may have to move into action on those previously impossible dreams.

Life is what we make of it. Whether we conceive of an inner god force or an other, outer God, doesn't matter. Relying on that force does.

"Ask and you shall receive. Knock and it shall be opened to you. . . ." These words are among the more unpleasant ones ascribed to Jesus Christ. They suggest the possibility of scientific method: ask (experiment) and see what happens (record the results).

Is it any wonder we discount answered prayers? We call it coincidence. We call it luck. We call it anything but what it is— the hand of God, or good, activated by our own hand when we act in behalf of our truest dreams, when we commit to our own soul.

Even the most timid life contains such moments of commitment: "I will get a new love seat after all!" And then, "I found the perfect one. It was the strangest thing. I was at my Aunt Bernice's and her neighbor was having a garage sale and she had this wonderful love seat her new husband was allergic to!"

In outsized lives, such moments stand out in bas-relief, large as Mount Rushmore: Lewis and Clark headed west. Isak Dinesen took off for Africa. We all have our Africas, those dark and romantic notions that call to our deepest selves. When we answer that call, when we commit to it, we set in motion the principle that C. G. Jung dubbed *synchronicity,* loosely defined as a fortuitous intermeshing of events. Back in the sixties, we called it *serendipity.* Whatever you choose to call it, once you begin your creative recovery you may be startled to find it cropping up everywhere.

Don't be surprised if you try to discount it. It can be a very threatening concept. Although Jung's paper on synchronicity was a cornerstone of his thought, even many Jungians prefer to believe it was a sort of side issue. They dismiss it, like his interest in the I Ching, as an oddity, nothing to take too seriously.

Jung might differ with them. Following his own inner leadings brought him to experience and describe a phenomenon that some of us prefer to ignore: the possibility of an intelligent and responsive universe, acting and reacting in our interests.

It is my experience that this *is* the case. I have learned, as a rule of thumb, never to ask whether you can do something. Say, instead, that you are doing it. Then fasten your seat belt. The most remarkable things follow.

"God is efficient," the actress Julianna McCarthy always reminds me. I have many times marveled at the sleight of hand with which the universe delivers its treats.

About six years ago, a play of mine was chosen for a large staged reading at the Denver Center for the Performing Arts. I had written the play with my friend Julianna in mind for the lead. She was my ideal casting, but when I arrived in Denver, casting was already set. As soon as I met my leading lady, I had a funny feeling there was a bomb ticking. I mentioned this to the director but was assured the actress was a consummate professional. Still, the funny feeling lingered in my stomach. Sure enough, a week before we were set to open, our leading lady abruptly resigned—from my play and from *Painting Churches,* the play that was in mid-run.

The Denver Center was stunned and very apologetic. They felt terrible about the damage my play would sustain by the abrupt departure. "In a perfect world, who would you cast?" they asked me. I told them, "Julianna McCarthy."

Julianna was hired and flown in from Los Angeles. No sooner did the center's directors lay eyes on her work than they asked her not only to do my play but also to take over the run of *Painting Churches*—for which she was brilliantly cast.

"God is showing off," I laughed to Julianna, very happy that she had the chance to do "her" play after all.

In my experience, the universe falls in with worthy plans and most especially with festive and expansive ones. I have

Chance is always powerful. Let your hook be always cast; in the pool where you least expect it, there will be a fish.

OVID

seldom conceived a delicious plan without being given the means to accomplish it. Understand that the *what* must come before the *how*. First choose *what* you would do. The *how* usually falls into place of itself.

All too often, when people talk about creative work, they emphasize strategy. Neophytes are advised of the Machiavellian devices they must employ to break into the field. I think this is a lot of rubbish. If you ask an artist how he got where he is, he will not describe breaking in but instead will talk of a series of lucky breaks. "A thousand unseen helping hands," Joseph Campbell calls these breaks. I call them synchronicity. It is my contention that you can count on them.

Remember that creativity is a tribal experience and that tribal elders will initiate the gifted youngsters who cross their path. This may sound like wishful thinking, but it is not. Sometimes an older artist will be moved to help out even against his or her own wishes. "I don't know why I'm doing this for you, but . . ." Again, I would say that some of the helping hands may be something more than human.

We like to pretend it is hard to follow our heart's dreams. The truth is, it is difficult to avoid walking through the many doors that will open. Turn aside your dream and it will come back to you again. Get willing to follow it again and a second mysterious door will swing open.

The universe is prodigal in its support. We are miserly in what we accept. All gift horses are looked in the mouth and usually returned to sender. We say we are scared by failure, but what frightens us more is the possibility of success.

Take a small step in the direction of a dream and watch the synchronous doors flying open. Seeing, after all, is believing. And if you see the results of your experiments, you will not need to believe me. Remember the maxim "Leap, and the net will appear." In his book, *The Scottish Himalayan Expedition*, W. H. Murray tells us his explorer's experience:

> Until one is committed, there is hesitancy, the chance to draw back, always ineffectiveness. Concerning all acts of initiative [or creation] there is one elementary truth, the ignorance of which kills countless ideas and splendid

Desire, ask, believe, receive.

Stella Terrill Mann

plans: that the moment one definitely commits oneself, then Providence moves too.

All sorts of things occur to help one that would otherwise never have occurred. A whole stream of events issues from the decision, raising in one's favor all manner of incidents and meetings and material assistance which no man would have believed would have come his way.

If you do not trust Murray —or me— you might want to trust Goethe. Statesman, scholar, artist, man of the world. Goethe had this to say on the will of Providence assisting our efforts:

> Whatever you think you can do or believe you can do, begin it. Action has magic, grace, and power in it.

Genuine beginnings begin within us, even when they are brought to our attention by external opportunities.

WILLIAM BRIDGES

SHAME

Some of you are thinking, "If it were that easy to take an action, I wouldn't be reading this book." Those of us who get bogged down by fear before action are usually being sabotaged by an older enemy, shame. Shame is a controlling device. Shaming someone is an attempt to prevent the person from behaving in a way that embarrasses us.

Making a piece of art may feel a lot like telling a family secret. Secret telling, by its very nature, involves shame and fear. It asks the question "What will they think of me once they know this?" This is a frightening question, particularly if we have ever been made to feel ashamed for our curiosities and explorations—social, sexual, spiritual.

"How dare you?" angry adults often rage at an innocent child who has stumbled onto a family secret. (How dare you open your mother's jewelry box? How dare you open your father's desk drawer? How dare you open the bedroom door? How dare you go down in the cellar, up in the attic, into some dark place where we hide those things we don't want you to know?)

The act of making art exposes a society to itself. Art brings things to light. It illuminates us. It sheds light on our lingering darkness. It casts a beam into the heart of our own darkness and says, "See?"

When people do not want to see something, they get mad at the one who shows them. They kill the messenger. A child from an alcoholic home gets into trouble scholastically or sexually. The family is flagged as being troubled. The child is made to feel shame for bringing shame to the family. But did the child bring shame? No. The child brought shameful things to light. The family shame predated and caused the child's distress. "What will the neighbors think?" is a shaming device aimed at continuing a conspiracy of illness.

Art opens the closets, airs out the cellars and attics. It brings healing. But before a wound can heal it must be seen, and this act of exposing the wound to air and light, the artist's act, is often reacted to with shaming. Bad reviews are a prime source of shame for many artists. The truth is, many reviews do aim at creating shame in an artist. "Shame on you! How dare you make that rotten piece of art?"

For the artist who endured childhood shaming—over any form of neediness, any type of exploration, any expectation— shame may kick in even without the aid of a shame-provoking review. If a child has ever been made to feel foolish for believing himself or herself talented, the act of actually finishing a piece of art will be fraught with internal shaming.

Many artists begin a piece of work, get well along in it, and then find, as they near completion, that the work seems mysteriously drained of merit. It's no longer worth the trouble. To therapists, this surge of sudden disinterest ("It doesn't matter") is a routine coping device employed to deny pain and ward off vulnerability.

Adults who grew up in dysfunctional homes learn to use this coping device very well. They call it detachment, but it is actually a numbing out.

"He forgot my birthday. Oh, well, no big deal."

A lifetime of this kind of experience, in which needs for recognition are routinely dishonored, teaches a young child that putting anything out for attention is a dangerous act.

"Dragging home the invisible bone" is how one recovering artist characterized her vain search for an achievement big enough to gain approval in her family of origin. "No matter how big a deal it was, they never seemed to take much notice.

The cost of a thing is the amount of what I call life which is required to be exchanged for it, immediately or in the long run.

HENRY DAVID THOREAU

They always found something wrong with it. All A's and one B and that B got the attention."

It is only natural that a young artist try to flag parental attention by way of accomplishments—positive or negative. Faced with indifference or rage, such youngsters soon learn that no bone would really meet with parental approval.

Often we are wrongly shamed as creatives. From this shaming we learn that we are wrong to create. Once we learn this lesson, we forget it instantly. Buried under *it doesn't matter,* the shame lives on, waiting to attach itself to our new efforts. The very act of attempting to make art creates shame.

This is why many a great student film is never sent off to festivals where it can be seen; why good novels are destroyed or live in desk drawers. This is why plays do not get sent out, why talented actors don't audition. This is why artists may feel shame at admitting their dreams. Shame is retriggered in us as adults because our internal artist is always our creative child. Because of this, making a piece of art may cause us to feel shame.

We don't make art with its eventual criticism foremost in mind, but criticism that asks a question like "How could you?" can make an artist feel like a shamed child. A well-meaning friend who constructively criticizes a beginning writer may very well end that writer.

Let me be clear. Not all criticism is shaming. In fact, even the most severe criticism when it fairly hits the mark is apt to be greeted by an internal *Ah-hah!* if it shows the artist a new and valid path for work. The criticism that damages is that which disparages, dismisses, ridicules, or condemns. It is frequently vicious but vague and difficult to refute. This is the criticism that damages.

Shamed by such criticism, an artist may become blocked or stop sending work out into the world. A perfectionist friend, teacher, or critic—like a perfectionist parent who nitpicks at missing commas—can dampen the ardor of a young artist who is just learning to let it rip. Because of this, as artists, we must learn to be very self-protective.

Does this mean no criticism? No. It means learning where and when to seek out right criticism. As artists, we must learn

We will discover the nature of our particular genius when we stop trying to conform to our own or to other peoples' models, learn to be ourselves, and allow our natural channel to open.

SHAKTI GAWAIN

when criticism is appropriate and from whom. Not only the source but the timing is very important here. A first draft is seldom appropriately shown to any but the most gentle and discerning eye. It often takes another artist to see the embryonic work that is trying to sprout. The inexperienced or harsh critical eye, instead of nurturing the shoot of art into being, may shoot it down instead.

As artists, we cannot control all the criticism we will receive. We cannot make our professional critics more healthy or more loving or more constructive than they are. But we can learn to comfort our artist child over unfair criticism; we can learn to find friends with whom we can safely vent our pain. We can learn not to deny and stuff our feelings when we have been artistically savaged.

Art requires a safe hatchery. Ideally, artists find this first in their family, then in their school, and finally in a community of friends and supporters. This ideal is seldom a reality. As artists, we must learn to create our own safe environments. We must learn to protect our artist child from shame. We do this by defusing our childhood shamings, getting them on the page, and sharing them with a trusted, nonshaming other.

By telling our shame secrets around our art and telling them through our art, we release ourselves and others from darkness. This release is not always welcomed.

We must learn that when our art reveals a secret of the human soul, those watching it may try to shame us for making it.

"It's terrible!" they may say, attacking the work when the work itself is actually fine. This can be very confusing. When we are told, "Shame on you" and feel it, we must learn to recognize this shame as a re-creation of childhood shames.

"I know that work is good. . . . I thought that was good work. . . . Could I be kidding myself? . . . Maybe that critic is right. . . . Why did I ever have the nerve to think. . . ?" And the downward spiral begins.

At these times, we must be very firm with ourselves and not pick up the first doubt. We simply cannot allow the first negative thinking to take hold. Taking in the first doubt is like picking up the first drink for an alcoholic. Once in our system, the doubt will take on another doubt—and another. Doubting thoughts can be stopped, but it takes vigilance to do it. "Maybe that critic was right. . . ." And, *boom,* we must go into action: "You are a good artist, a brave artist, you are doing well. It's good that you did the work. . . ."

When *God's Will,* the romantic film comedy I directed, debuted in Washington, D.C., it was a homecoming for me. My earliest journalism work had been for the *Washington Post.* I was hoping for a hometown-girl-makes-good reception. But in the reviews printed prior to the opening, I did not get it.

The Post sent a young woman who watched an entire movie about theater people and then wrote that it was about movie people. She added that "Most" of my dialogue had been *stolen* from "Casablanca." I wondered what movie she had seen; not the one I made. My movie had forty odd theater jokes and a one line joke about "Casablanca." Those were the facts but they didn't do me any good.

I was mortified. Shamed. Ready to (almost) die.

Because the antidote for shame is self-love and self-praise, this is what I did. I went for a walk through Rock Creek Park. I prayed. I made a list for myself of past compliments and good reviews. I did not tell myself, "It doesn't matter." But I did tell my artist self, "You will heal."

And I showed up for my opening. It was a lot more successful than my reviews.

Three months later, my film was chosen for a prestigious European festival. They offered to fly me over. To pay my expenses. To showcase my film. I hesitated. The Washington shaming had done its slow and poisonous work. I was afraid to go.

But I knew better than to not go. My years in artistic recovery had taught me to just show up. When I did, my film sold at a great price and won a headline in *Variety.*

I share the headline because the irony of it was not lost on me. "*God's Will* Hit in Munich," it read.

It *is* "God's will" for us to be creative.

What doesn't kill me makes me stronger.

ALBERT CAMUS

DEALING WITH CRITICISM

It is important to be able to sort useful criticism from the other kind. Often we need to do the sorting out for ourselves, without the benefit of a public vindication. As artists, we are far more able to do this sorting than people might suspect. Pointed criticism, if accurate, often gives the artist an inner sense of relief: "Ah, hah! so that's what was wrong with it." Useful criticism ultimately leaves us with one more puzzle piece for our work.

The words that enlighten the soul are more precious than jewels.

HAZRAT INAYAT KHAN

Useless criticism, on the other hand, leaves us with a feeling of being bludgeoned. As a rule, it is withering and shaming in tone; ambiguous in content; personal, inaccurate, or blanket in its condemnations. There is nothing to be gleaned from irresponsible criticism.

You are dealing with an inner child. Artistic child abuse creates rebellion creates block. All that can be done with abusive criticism is to heal from it.

There are certain rules of the road useful in dealing with *any* form of criticism.

1. Receive the criticism all the way through and get it over with.

2. Jot down notes to yourself on what concepts or phrases bother you.

3. Jot down notes on what concepts or phrases seem useful.

4. Do something very nurturing for yourself—read an old good review or recall a compliment.

5. Remember that even if you have made a truly rotten piece of art, it may be a *necessary* stepping-stone to your next work. Art matures spasmodically and *requires* ugly-duckling growth stages.

6. Look at the criticism again. Does it remind you of any criticism from your past—particularly shaming childhood criticism? Acknowledge to yourself that the cur-

rent criticism is triggering grief over a long-standing wound.

7. Write a letter to the critic—not to be mailed, most probably. Defend your work *and* acknowledge what was helpful, if anything, in the criticism proffered.

8. Get back on the horse. Make an immediate commitment to do something creative.

9. Do it. Creativity is the only cure for criticism.

DETECTIVE WORK, AN EXERCISE

Many blocked people are actually very powerful and creative personalities who have been made to feel guilty about their own strengths and gifts. Without being acknowledged, they are often used as batteries by their families and friends, who feel free to both use their creative energies and disparage them. When these blocked artists strive to break free of their dysfunctional systems, they are often urged to be sensible when such advice is not appropriate for them. Made to feel guilty for their talents, they often hide their own light under a bushel for fear of hurting others. Instead, they hurt themselves.

A little sleuth work is in order to restore the persons we have abandoned—ourselves. When you complete the following phrases, you may feel strong emotion as you retrieve memories and misplaced fragments of yourself. Allow yourself to free-associate for a sentence or so with each phrase.

1. My favorite childhood toy was . . .

2. My favorite childhood game was . . .

3. The best movie I ever saw as a kid was . . .

4. I don't do it much but I enjoy . . .

5. If I could lighten up a little, I'd let myself . . .

6. If it weren't too late, I'd . . .

7. My favorite musical instrument is . . .

Artists who seek perfection in everything are those who cannot attain it in anything.

EUGÈNE DELACROIX

8. The amount of money I spend on treating myself to entertainment each month is . . .

9. If I weren't so stingy with my artist, I'd buy him/her . . .

10. Taking time out for myself is . . .

11. I am afraid that if I start dreaming . . .

12. I secretly enjoy reading . . .

13. If I had had a perfect childhood I'd have grown up to be . . .

14. If it didn't sound so crazy, I'd write or make a . . .

15. My parents think artists are . . .

16. My God thinks artists are . . .

17. What makes me feel weird about this recovery is . . .

18. Learning to trust myself is probably . . .

19. My most cheer-me-up music is . . .

20. My favorite way to dress is . . .

Take your life in your own hands and what happens? A terrible thing: no one to blame.

ERICA JONG

GROWTH

Growth is an erratic forward movement: two steps forward, one step back. Remember that and be very gentle with yourself. A creative recovery is a healing process. You are capable of great things on Tuesday, but on Wednesday you may slide backward. This is normal. Growth occurs in spurts. You will lie dormant sometimes. Do not be discouraged. Think of it as resting.

Very often, a week of insights will be followed by a week of sluggishness. The morning pages will seem pointless. *They are not.* What you are learning to do, writing them even when you are tired and they seem dull, is to rest on the page. This is very important. Marathon runners suggest you log ten slow miles for every fast one. The same holds true for creativity.

In this sense, *Easy does it* is actually a modus operandi. It means, "Easy accomplishes it." If you will hew to a practice of writing three pages every morning and doing one kind thing for yourself every day, you will begin to notice a slight lightness of heart.

Practice being kind to yourself in small, concrete ways. Look at your refrigerator. Are you feeding yourself nicely? Do you have socks? An extra set of sheets? What about a new house plant? A thermos for the long drive to work? Allow yourself to pitch out some of your old ragged clothes. You don't have to keep everything.

The expression "God helps those who help themselves" may take on a new and very different meaning. Where in the past it translated, "God helps only those who earn help," it will now come to signify the amazing number of small free gifts the creator showers on those who are helping themselves to a little bounty. If you do one nice thing a day for yourself, God will do two more. Be alert for support and encouragement from unexpected quarters. Be open to receiving gifts from odd channels: free tickets, a free trip, an offer to buy you dinner, a new-to-you old couch. Practice saying yes to such help.

The scientifically inclined among you might want to make a good, thorough list of clothes you wish you had. Very often, the items on the list come into your possession at disconcerting speed. Just try it. Experiment.

More than anything else, experiment with solitude. You will need to make a commitment to quiet time. Try to acquire the habit of checking in with yourself. Several times a day, just take a beat, and ask yourself how *you* are feeling. Listen to your answer. Respond kindly. If you are doing something very hard, promise yourself a break and a treat afterward.

Yes, I *am* asking you to baby yourself. We believe that to be artists we must be tough, cynical, and intellectually chilly. Leave that to the critics. As a creative being, you will be more productive when coaxed than when bullied.

There is a vitality, a life force, an energy, a quickening, that is translated through you into action, and because there is only one of you in all time, this expression is unique. And if you block it, it will never exist through any other medium and will be lost.

MARTHA GRAHAM

TASKS ✉

1. Describe your childhood room. If you wish, you may sketch this room. What was your favorite thing

*Whenever I have to choose be-
tween two evils, I always like
to try the one I haven't tried
before.*

MAE WEST

about it? What's your favorite thing about your room right now? Nothing? Well, get something you like in there—maybe something from that old childhood room.

2. Describe five traits you like in yourself as a child.

3. List five childhood accomplishments. (straight A's in seventh grade, trained the dog, punched out the class bully, short-sheeted the priest's bed).

   And a treat: list five favorite childhood foods. Buy yourself one of them this week. Yes, Jell-O with bananas is okay.

4. Habits: Take a look at your habits. Many of them may interfere with your self-nurturing and cause shame. Some of the oddest things are self-destructive. Do you have a habit of watching TV you don't like? Do you have a habit of hanging out with a really boring friend and just killing time (there's an expression!)? Some rotten habits are obvious, overt (drinking too much, smoking, eating instead of writing). List three obvious rotten habits. What's the payoff in continuing them?

   Some rotten habits are more subtle (no time to exercise, little time to pray, always helping others, not getting any self-nurturing, hanging out with people who belittle your dreams). List three of your subtle foes. What use do these forms of sabotage have? Be specific.

5. Make a list of friends who nurture you—that's *nurture* (give you a sense of your own competency and possibility), not enable (give you the message that you will never get it straight without their help). There is a big difference between being helped and being treated as though we are helpless. List three nurturing friends. Which of their traits, particularly, serve you well?

6. Call a friend who treats you like you are a really good and bright person who can accomplish things. Part

of your recovery is reaching out for support. This support will be critical as you undertake new risks.

7. Inner Compass: Each of us has an inner compass. This is an instinct that points us toward health. It warns us when we are on dangerous ground, and it tells us when something is safe and good for us. Morning pages are one way to contact it. So are some other artist-brain activities—painting, driving, walking, scrubbing, running. This week, take an hour to follow your inner compass by doing an artist-brain activity and *listening* to what insights bubble up.

8. List five people you admire. Now, list five people you secretly admire. What traits do these people have that you can cultivate further in yourself?

9. List five people you wish you had met who are dead. Now, list five people who are dead whom you'd like to hang out with for a while in eternity. What traits do you find in these people that you can look for in your friends?

10. Compare the two sets of lists. Take a look at what you really like and really admire—and a look at what you think you should like and admire. Your *shoulds* might tell you to admire Edison while your heart belongs to Houdini. Go with the Houdini side of you for a while.

Creative work is play. It is free speculation using the materials of one's chosen form.

STEPHEN
NACHMANOVITCH

Creativity is . . . seeing something that doesn't exist already. You need to find out how you can bring it into being and that way be a playmate with God.

MICHELE SHEA

CHECK-IN ✎

1. How many days this week did you do your morning pages? How was the experience for you? If you skipped a day, why did you skip it?

2. Did you do your artist date this week? (Yes, yes, and it was *awful.*) What did you do? How did it feel?

3. Did you experience any synchronicity this week? What was it?

4. Were there any other issues this week that you consider significant for your recovery? Describe them.

Recovering a Sense of Integrity

This week may find you grappling with changing self-definition. The essays, tasks, and exercises are designed to catapult you into productive introspection and integration of new self-awareness. This may be both very difficult and extremely exciting for you. Warning: Do not skip the tool of reading deprivation!

HONEST CHANGES

WORKING WITH THE MORNING pages, we begin to sort through the differences between our *real* feelings, which are often secret, and our *official* feelings, those on the record for public display. Official feelings are often indicated by the phrase, "I feel okay about that [the job loss, her dating someone else, my dad's death, . . .]."

What do we mean by "I feel okay"? The morning pages force us to get specific. Does "I feel okay" mean I feel resigned, accepting, comfortable, detached, numb, tolerant, pleased, or satisfied? *What* does it mean?

Okay is a blanket word for most of us. It covers all sorts of squirmy feelings; and it frequently signals a loss. We officially feel okay, but do we?

At the root of a successful creative recovery is the commitment to puncture our denial, to stop saying, "It's okay" when in fact it's something else. The morning pages press us to answer what else.

In my years of watching people work with morning pages,

Each painting has its own way of evolving. . . . When the painting is finished, the subject reveals itself.

WILLIAM BAZIOTES

I have noticed that many tend to neglect or abandon the pages whenever an unpleasant piece of clarity is about to emerge. If we are, for example, very, very angry but not admitting it, then we will be tempted to say we feel "okay about that." The morning pages will not allow us to get away with this evasion. So we tend to avoid them.

If we have the creeping feeling that our lover is not being totally honest with us, the morning pages are liable to bring this creepy possibility up—and with it, the responsibility for an unsettling conversation. Rather than face this mess, we will mess up on doing the morning pages.

By contrast, if we are suddenly and madly in love, the morning pages may seem threatening. We don't want to puncture the fragile and shiny bubble of our happiness. We want to stay lost in the sea of a blissful us rather than be reminded that there is an I in the we (or an "eye" in the we) that is temporarily blinded.

In short, extreme emotions of any kind—the very thing that morning pages are superb for processing—are the usual triggers for avoiding the pages themselves.

Just as an athlete accustomed to running becomes irritable when he is unable to get his miles in, so, too, those of us accustomed now to morning pages will notice an irritability when we let them slide. We are tempted, always, to reverse cause and effect: "I was too crabby to write them," instead of, "I didn't write them so I am crabby."

Over any considerable period of time, the morning pages perform spiritual chiropractic. They realign our values. If we are to the left or the right of our personal truth, the pages will point out the need for a course adjustment. We will become aware of our drift and correct it—if only to hush the pages up.

"To thine own self be true," the pages say, while busily pointing that self out. It was in the pages that Mickey, a painter, first learned she wanted to write comedy. No wonder all her friends were writers. So was she!

Chekhov advised, "If you want to work on your art, work on your life." That's another way of saying that in order to have self-expression, we must first have a self to express. That is the business of the morning pages: "I, myself, feel this way . . .

and that way . . . and this way. . . . No one else need agree
with me, but this is what *I* feel."

The process of identifying a *self* inevitably involves loss as
well as gain. We discover our boundaries, and those boundaries by definition separate us from our fellows. As we clarify
our perceptions, we lose our misconceptions. As we eliminate
ambiguity, we lose illusion as well. We arrive at clarity, and
clarity creates change.

"I have outgrown this job," may appear in the morning
pages. At first, it is a troubling perception. Over time, it becomes a call for action and then an action plan.

"This marriage is not working for me," the morning pages
say. And then, "I wonder about couples therapy?" And then,
"I wonder if I'm not just bored with me?"

In addition to posing problems, the pages may also pose
solutions. "I *am* bored with me. It would be fun to learn
French." Or, "I noticed a sign just down the block for a clay and
fiber class. That sounds interesting."

As we notice which friends bore us, which situations leave
us stifled, we are often rocked by waves of sorrow. We may
want our illusions back! We want to pretend the friendship
works. We don't want the trauma of searching for another job.

Faced with impending change, change we have set in motion through our own hand, we want to mutiny, curl up in a
ball, bawl our eyes out. "No pain, no gain," the nasty slogan
has it. And we resent this pain no matter what gain it is bringing us.

"I don't want to raise my consciousness!" we wail. "I
want . . ." And thanks to the morning pages we learn what we
want and ultimately become willing to make the changes
needed to get it. But not without a tantrum. And not without a
kriya, a Sanskrit word meaning a spiritual emergency or surrender. (I always think of kriyas as spiritual seizures. Perhaps
they should be spelled *crias* because they are cries of the soul as
it is wrung through changes.)

We all know what a kriya looks like: it is the bad case of the
flu right after you've broken up with your lover. It's the rotten
head cold and bronchial cough that announces you've abused
your health to meet an unreachable work deadline. That asthma

Eliminate something superfluous from your life. Break a habit. Do something that makes you feel insecure.

PIERO FERRUCCI

attack out of nowhere when you've just done a round of care-taking your alcoholic sibling? That's a kriya, too.

Always significant, frequently psychosomatic, kriyas are the final insult our psyche adds to our injuries: "Get it?" a kriya asks you.

Get it:

Stop thinking and talking about it and there is nothing you will not be able to know.

ZEN PARADIGM

You can't stay with this abusive lover.

You can't work at a job that demands eighty hours a week.

You can't rescue a brother who needs to save himself.

In twelve-step groups, kriyas are often called *surrenders*. People are told *just let go.* And they would if they knew what they were holding on to. With the morning pages in place and the artist dates in motion, the radio set stands half a chance of picking up the message you are sending and/or receiving. The pages round up the usual suspects. They mention the small hurts we prefer to ignore, the large successes we've failed to ac-knowledge. In short, the morning pages point the way to real-ity: this is how you're feeling; what do you make of that?

And what we make of that is often art.

People frequently believe the creative life is grounded in fantasy. The more difficult truth is that creativity is grounded in reality, in the particular, the focused, the well observed or specifically imagined.

As we lose our vagueness about our self, our values, our life situation, we become available to the moment. It is there, in the particular, that we contact the creative self. Until we expe-rience the freedom of solitude, we cannot connect authen-tically. We may be enmeshed, but we are not encountered.

Art lies in the moment of encounter: we meet our truth and we meet ourselves; we meet ourselves and we meet our self-expression. We become original because we become something specific: an origin from which work flows.

As we gain—or regain—our creative identity, we lose the false self we were sustaining. The loss of this false self can feel traumatic: "I don't know who I am anymore. I don't recog-nize me."

Remember that the more you feel yourself to be terra incognita, the more certain you can be that the recovery process is working. You are your own promised land, your own new frontier.

Shifts in taste and perception frequently accompany shifts in identity. One of the clearest signals that something healthy is afoot is the impulse to weed out, sort through, and discard old clothes, papers, and belongings.

"I don't need this anymore," we say as we toss a low-self-worth shirt into the giveaway pile. "I'm sick of this broken-down dresser and its sixteen coats of paint," as the dresser goes off to Goodwill.

By tossing out the old and unworkable, we make way for the new and suitable. A closet stuffed with ratty old clothes does not invite new ones. A house overflowing with odds and ends and tidbits you've held on to for someday has no space for the things that might truly enhance today.

When the search-and-discard impulse seizes you, two crosscurrents are at work: the old you is leaving and grieving, while the new you celebrates and grows strong. As with any rupture, there is both tension and relief. Long-seated depression breaks up like an ice floe. Long-frozen feelings thaw, melt, cascade, flood, and often overrun their container (you). You may find yourself feeling volatile and changeable. You are.

Be prepared for bursts of tears and of laughter. A certain giddiness may accompany sudden stabs of loss. Think of yourself as an accident victim walking away from the crash: your old life has crashed and burned; your new life isn't apparent yet. You may feel yourself to be temporarily without a vehicle. Just keep walking.

If this description sounds dramatic, it is only to prepare you for possible emotional pyrotechnics. You may not have them. Your changes may be more like cloud movements, from overcast to partly cloudy. It is important to know that no matter which form your growth takes, there is another kind of change, slower and more subtle, accumulating daily whether you sense its presence or not.

"Nothing dramatic is happening to me. I don't think the process is working," I have often been told by someone who

All the arts we practice are apprenticeship. The big art is our life.

M. C. RICHARDS

It is not because things are difficult that we do not dare; it is because we do not dare that they are difficult.

SENECA

To become truly immortal, a work of art must escape all human limits: logic and common sense will only interfere. But once these barriers are broken, it will enter the realms of childhood visions and dreams.

GIORGIO DE CHIRICO

from my perspective is changing at the speed of light. The analogy that I use is that once we engage in the process of morning pages and artist dates, we begin to move at such velocity that we do not even realize the pace. Just as travelers on a jet are seldom aware of their speed unless they hit a patch of turbulence, so, too, travelers on the Artist's Way are seldom aware of the speed of their growth. This is a form of denial that can tempt us to abort the recovery process that "isn't happening" to us. Oh yes it is.

When we have engaged the creator within to heal us, many changes and shifts in our attitudes begin to occur. I enumerate some of them here because many of these will not be recognizable at first as healing. If fact, they may seem crazy and even destructive. At best, they will seem eccentric.

There will be a change in energy patterns. Your dreams will become stronger and clearer, both by night and by day. You will find yourself remembering your nighttime dreams, and by day, daydreams will catch your attention. Fantasy, of a benign and unexpected sort, will begin to crop up.

Many areas of your life that previously seemed to fit will stop fitting. Half your wardrobe may start to look funny. You may decide to reupholster a couch or just toss it out. Musical bents may alter. There may even be bursts of spontaneous singing, dancing, running.

You may find your candor unsettling. "I don't like that" is a sentence that will leave your mouth. Or "I think that's great." In short, your tastes and judgments and personal identity will begin to show through.

What you have been doing is wiping the mirror. Each day's morning pages take a swipe at the blur you have kept between you and your real self. As your image becomes clearer, it may surprise you. You may discover very particular likes and dislikes that you hadn't acknowledged. A fondness for cactuses. So why do I have these pots of ivy? A dislike for brown. So why do I keep wearing that sweater if I never feel right in it?

Conditioned as we are to accept other peoples' definitions of us, this emerging individuality can seem to us like self-will run riot. It is not.

The snowflake pattern of your soul is emerging. Each of us is a unique, creative individual. But we often blur that uniqueness with sugar, alcohol, drugs, overwork, underplay, bad relations, toxic sex, underexercise, over-TV, undersleep—many and varied forms of junk food for the soul. The pages help us to see these smears on our consciousness.

Is you look over the time you have been doing your morning writing, you will see that many changes have entered your life as a result of your willingness to clear room in it for your creator's action. You will have noticed an increased, sometimes disconcerting, sense of personal energy, some bursts of anger, some flash points of clarity. People and objects may have taken on a different meaning to you. There will be a sense of the flow of life—that you are brought into new vistas as you surrender to moving with the flow of God. This is clear already.

You may well be experiencing a sense of both bafflement and faith. You are no longer stuck, but you cannot tell where you are going. You may feel that this can't keep up. You may long for the time when there was no sense of possibility, when you felt more victimized, when you didn't realize how many small things you could do to improve your own life.

It is normal to yearn for some rest when you are moving so rapidly. What you will learn to do is rest in motion, like lying down in a boat. Your morning pages are your boat. They will both lead you forward and give you a place to recuperate from your forward motion.

It is difficult for us to realize that this process of going inside and writing pages can open an inner door through which our creator helps and guides us. Our willingness swings this inner door open. The morning pages symbolize our willingness to speak to and hear God. They lead us into many other changes that also come from God and lead us to God. This is the hand of God moving through your hand as you write. It is very powerful.

One technique that can be very reassuring at this point is to use your morning pages—or a part of them—for written affirmation of your progress.

"Put it in writing," we often say when making a deal.

The center that I cannot find is known to my unconscious mind.

W. H. AUDEN

All you need to do to receive guidance is to ask for it and then listen.

SANAYA ROMAN

There is a special power in writing out the deal we are making with our creator. "I receive your good willingly" and "Thy will be done" are two short affirmations that when written in the morning remind us to be open to increased good during the day.

"I trust my perceptions" is another powerful affirmation to use as we undergo shifts in identity. "A stronger and clearer me is emerging."

Choose affirmations according to your need. As you excavate your buried dreams, you need the assurance that such explorations are permissible: "I recover and enjoy my identity."

BURIED DREAMS, AN EXERCISE

As recovering creatives, we often have to excavate our own pasts for the shards of buried dreams and delights. Do a little digging, please. Be fast and frivolous. This is an exercise in spontaneity, so be sure to write your answers out quickly. Speed kills the Censor.

1. List five hobbies that sound fun.

2. List five classes that sound fun.

3. List five things you personally would *never* do that sound fun.

4. List five skills that would be fun to have.

5. List five things you used to enjoy doing.

6. List five silly things you would like to try once.

As you may have gathered by this point in your work, we will approach certain problems from many different angles, all of them aimed at eliciting more information from your unconscious about what you might consciously enjoy. The exercise that follows will teach you enormous amounts about yourself—as well as giving you some free time in which to pursue the interests you just listed.

READING DEPRIVATION

If you feel stuck in your life or in your art, few jump starts are more effective than a week of *reading deprivation*.

No reading? That's right: no reading. For most artists, words are like tiny tranquilizers. We have a daily quota of media chat that we swallow up. Like greasy food, it clogs our system. Too much of it and we feel, yes, fried.

It is a paradox that by emptying our lives of distractions we are actually filling the well. Without distractions, we are once again thrust into the sensory world. With no newspaper to shield us, a train becomes a viewing gallery. With no novel to sink into (and no television to numb us out) an evening becomes a vast savannah in which furniture—and other assumptions—get rearranged.

Reading deprivation casts us into our inner silence, a space some of us begin to immediately fill with new words—long, gossipy conversations, television bingeing, the radio as a constant, chatty companion. We often cannot hear our own inner voice, the voice of our artist's inspiration, above the static. In practicing reading deprivation, we need to cast a watchful eye on these other pollutants. They poison the well.

If we monitor the inflow and keep it to a minimum, we will be rewarded for our reading deprivation with embarrassing speed. Our reward will be a new outflow. Our own art, our own thoughts and feelings, will begin to nudge aside the sludge of blockage, to loosen it and move it upward and outward until once again our well is running freely.

Reading deprivation is a very powerful tool—and a very frightening one. Even thinking about it can bring up enormous rage. For most blocked creatives, reading is an addiction. We gobble the words of others rather than digest our own thoughts and feelings, rather than cook up something of our own.

In my teaching, the week that I assign reading deprivation is always a tough one. I go to the podium knowing that I will be the enemy. I break the news that we won't be reading and then I brace myself for the waves of antagonism and sarcasm that follow.

We are always doing something, talking, reading, listening to the radio, planning what next. The mind is kept naggingly busy on some easy, unimportant external thing all day.

BRENDA UELAND

At least one student always explains to me—pointedly, in no uncertain terms—that he or she is a very important and busy person with duties and obligations that include reading.

This information is inevitably relayed in a withering tone that implies I am an idiot child, an artistic flake, unable to grasp the complexities of an adult's life. I just listen.

In a dark time, the eye begins to see.

THEODORE ROETHKE

When the rage has been vented, when all the assigned reading for college courses and jobs has been mentioned, I point out that I have had jobs and I have gone to college and that in my experience I had many times wriggled out of reading for a week due to procrastination. As blocked creatives, we can be very creative at wriggling out of things. I ask my class to turn their creativity to wriggling *into* not reading.

"But what will we do?" comes next.

Here is a brief list of some things that people do when they are not reading:

Listen to music.	Knit.	Work out.
Make curtains.	Cook.	Meditate.
Wash the dog.	Fix the bike.	Have friends to dinner.
Sort closets.	Watercolor.	Get the stereo working.
Pay bills.	Rewire the lamp.	
Write old friends.	Paint the bedroom.	Sort bookshelves (a dangerous one!).
Repot some plants.	Rearrange the kitchen.	Go dancing.
Mend.		

Even at the safe remove of the written word, I can feel the shock waves of antagonism about trying this tool. I will tell you that those who have most resisted it have come back the most smugly rewarded for having done it. The nasty bottom line is this: sooner or later, if you are not reading, you will run out of work and be forced to play. You'll light some incense or put on an old jazz record or paint a shelf turquoise, and then you will feel not just better but actually a little excited.

Don't read. If you can't think of anything else to do, cha-cha.

(Yes, you can read and do this week's tasks.)

TASKS ✉

1. Environment: Describe your ideal environment. Town? Country? Swank? Cozy? One paragraph. One image, drawn or clipped, that conveys this. What's your favorite season? Why? Go through some magazines and find an image of this. Or draw it. Place it near your working area.

2. Time Travel: Describe yourself at eighty. What did you do after fifty that you enjoyed? Be very specific. Now, write a letter from you at eighty to you at your current age. What would you tell yourself? What interests would you urge yourself to pursue? What dreams would you encourage?

3. Time Travel: Remember yourself at eight. What did you like to do? What were your favorite things? Now, write a letter from you at eight to you at your current age. What would you tell yourself?

4. Environment: Look at your house. Is there any room that you could make into a secret, private space for yourself? Convert the TV room? Buy a screen or hang a sheet and cordon off a section of some other room? This is your dream area. It should be decorated for fun and not as an office. All you really need is a chair or pillow, something to write on, some kind of little altar area for flowers and candles. This is to help you center on the fact that creativity is a spiritual, not an ego, issue.

5. Use your life pie (from Week One) to review your growth. Has that nasty tarantula changed shape yet? Haven't you been more active, less rigid, more expressive? Be careful not to expect too much too soon.

When the soul wishes to experience something she throws an image of the experience out before her and enters into her own image.

MEISTER ECKHART

I learned that the real creator was my inner Self, the Shakti. . . . That desire to do something is God inside talking through us.

MICHELE SHEA

That's *raising the jumps*. Growth must have time to solidify into health. One day at a time, you are building the habit patterns of a healthy artist. Easy does do it. List ongoing self-nurturing toys you could buy your artist: books on tape, magazine subscriptions, theater tickets, a bowling ball.

6. Write your own Artist's Prayer. (See pages 207–208.) Use it every day for a week.

7. An Extended Artist Date: Plan a small vacation for yourself. (One weekend day. Get ready to execute it.)

8. Open your closet. Throw out—or hand on, or donate—one low-self-worth outfit. (You know the outfit.) Make space for the new.

9. Look at one situation in your life that you feel you should change but haven't yet. What is the payoff for you in staying stuck?

10. If you break your reading deprivation, write about how you did it. In a tantrum? A slipup? A binge? How do you feel about it? Why?

CHECK-IN ✐

1. How many days this week did you do your morning pages? (Tantrums often show up as skipping the morning pages.) How was the experience for you?

2. Did you do your artist date this week? (Does your artist get to do more than rent a movie?) What did you do? How did it feel?

3. Did you experience any synchronicity this week? What was it?

4. Were there any other issues this week that you consider significant for your recovery? Describe them.

Recovering a Sense of Possibility

This week you are being asked to examine your payoffs in remaining stuck. You will explore how you curtail your own possibilities by placing limits on the good you can receive. You will examine the cost of settling for appearing good instead of being authentic. You may find yourself thinking about radical changes, no longer ruling out your growth by making others the cause of your constriction.

LIMITS

ONE OF THE CHIEF barriers to accepting God's generosity is our limited notion of what we are in fact able to accomplish. We may tune in to the voice of the creator within, hear a message—and then discount it as crazy or impossible. On the one hand, we take ourselves very seriously and don't want to look like idiots pursuing some patently grandiose scheme. On the other hand, we don't take ourselves—or God—seriously enough and so we define as grandiose many schemes that, with God's help, may fall well within our grasp.

Remembering that God is my source, we are in the spiritual position of having an unlimited bank account. Most of us never consider how powerful the creator really is. Instead, we draw very limited amounts of the power available to us. We decide how powerful God is for us. We unconsciously set a limit on how much God can give us or help us. We are stingy with ourselves. And if we receive a gift beyond our imagining, we often send it back.

Some of you may be thinking that this sounds like the magic-wand chapter: I pray and presto! Sometimes, that *is* how it will feel. More often, what we are talking about seems to be a conscious partnership in which we work along slowly and gradually, clearing away the wreckage of our negative patterning, clarifying the vision of what it is we want, learning to accept small pieces of that vision from whatever source and then, one day, presto! The vision seems to suddenly be in place. In other words, pray to catch the bus, then run as fast as you can.

For this to happen, first of all, we must believe that we are allowed to catch the bus. We come to recognize that God is unlimited in supply and that everyone has equal access. This begins to clear up guilt about having or getting too much. Since everyone can draw on the universal supply, we deprive no one with our abundance. If we learn to think of receiving God's good as being an act of worship—cooperating with God's plan to manifest goodness in our lives—we can begin to let go of having to sabotage ourselves.

One reason we are miserly with ourselves is scarcity thinking. We don't want our luck to run out. We don't want to overspend our spiritual abundance. Again, we are limiting our flow by anthropomorphizing God into a capricious parent figure. Remembering that God is our source, an energy flow that *likes* to extend itself, we become more able to tap our creative power effectively.

God has lots of money. God has lots of movie ideas, novel ideas, poems, songs, paintings, acting jobs. God has a supply of loves, friends, houses that are all available to us. By listening to the creator within, we are led to our right path. On that path, we find friends, lovers, money, and meaningful work. Very often, when we cannot seem to find an adequate supply, it is because we are insisting on a particular human source of supply. We must learn to let the flow manifest itself where it will—not where we *will* it.

Cara, a writer, spent far longer than she should remaining in an abusive agent relationship because she thought it would be creative suicide to sever that professional tie. The relationship was plagued with evasions, half-truths, delays. Cara hung in, afraid to let go of her agent's prestige. Finally, after a particularly abusive phone call, Cara wrote a letter severing the relationship. She felt as if she had just jumped into outer space. When her husband came home, she tearfully told him how she had sabotaged her career. He listened and then said, "A week ago, I was in this bookstore and the owner asked me if you had a good agent. He gave me this woman's name and number. Call her."

Tearfully, Cara acquiesced. She got on the phone and connected immediately to the new agent's sensibility. They have been working together, very successfully, ever since.

To my eye, this is a story not only of synchronicity but also of right-dependence on universe as source. Once Cara became willing to receive her good from whatever source it appeared in, she stopped being victimized.

I recently had a woman artist tell me that she got her new and excellent agent by using affirmations. Even after years of artistic recovery, I still have my cynical side that says, "*Mmm.*" It is as though we want to believe God can create the subatomic structure but is clueless when faced with how to aid or fix our painting, sculpture, writing, film.

I recognize that many will balk at the simplicity of this concept. "God doesn't run the movie business," we want to say. "CAA does." I want to sound a cautionary note here for all artists who put their creative lives into solely human hands. This can block your good.

The desire to be worldly, sophisticated, and smart often blocks our flow. We have ideas and opinions about where our good should come from. As a Hollywood screenwriter, I had many rueful conversations with other screenwriters about the fact that while our agents were often invaluable, we seemed to get an awful lot of breaks from places like "my next door neighbor," "my dentist's brother," or "somebody my wife went to college with." Those breaks are God the source in action.

I have said before that creativity is a spiritual issue. Any progress is made by leaps of faith, some small and some large. At first, we may want faith to take the first dance class, the first step toward learning a new medium. Later, we may want the

Look and you will find it—what is unsought will go undetected.

SOPHOCLES

It is within my power either to serve God or not to serve him. Serving him, I add to my own good and the good of the whole world. Not serving him, I forfeit my own good and deprive the world of that good, which was in my power to create.

LEO TOLSTOY

faith and the funds for further classes, seminars, a larger work space, a year's sabbatical. Later still, we may conceive an idea for a book, an artists' collective gallery space. As each idea comes to us, we must in good faith clear away our inner barriers to acting on it and then, on an outer level, take the concrete steps necessary to trigger our synchronous good.

If this still sounds airy fairy to you, ask yourself bluntly what next step you are evading. What dream are you discounting as impossible given your resources? What payoff are you getting for remaining stuck at this point in your expansion?

God as my source is a simple but completely effective plan for living. It removes negative dependency—and anxiety—from our lives by assuring us that God will provide. Our job is to listen for how.

One way we listen is by writing our morning pages. At night, before we fall asleep, we can list areas in which we need guidance. In the morning, writing on these same topics, we find ourselves seeing previously unseen avenues of approach. Experiment with this two-step process: ask for answers in the evening; listen for answers in the morning. Be open to all help.

FINDING THE RIVER

For four weeks now, we have been excavating our consciousness. We have seen how often we think negatively and fearfully, how frightening it has been for us to begin to believe that there might be a right place for us that we could attain by listening to our creative voice and following its guidance. We have begun to hope, and we have feared that hope.

The shift to spiritual dependency is a gradual one. We have been making this shift slowly and surely. With each day we become more true to ourselves, more open to the positive. To our surprise, this seems to be working in our human relationships. We find we are able to tell more of our truth, hear more of other people's truth, and encompass a far more kindly attitude toward both. We are becoming less judgmental of ourselves and others. How is this possible? The morning pages, a flow of stream of consciousness, gradually loosens our hold on fixed opinions and short-sighted views. We see that our moods, views, and insights are transitory. We acquire a sense of movement, a current of change in our lives. This current, or river, is a flow of grace moving us to our right livelihood, companions, destiny.

Dependence on the creator within is really freedom from all other dependencies. Paradoxically, it is also the only route to real intimacy with other human beings. Freed from our terrible fears of abandonment, we are able to live with more spontaneity. Freed from our constant demands for more and more reassurance, our fellows are able to love us back without feeling so burdened.

As we have listened to our artist child within, it has begun to feel more and more safe. Feeling safe, it speaks a little louder. Even on our worst days, a small, positive voice says, "You could still do this or it might be fun to do that. . . ."

Most of us find that as we work with the morning pages, we are rendered less rigid that we were. Recovery is the process of finding the river and saying yes to its flow, rapids and all. We startle ourselves by saying yes instead of no to opportunities. As we begin to pry ourselves loose from our old self-concepts, we find that our new, emerging self may enjoy all sorts of bizarre adventures.

Michelle, a hard-driving, dressed-for-success lawyer, enrolled in flamenco dancing lessons and loved them. Her house—formerly a sleek, careerist's high-tech showcase— suddenly began filling up with lush plants, plump pillows, sensuous incense. Tropical colors bloomed on the once-white walls. For the first time in years, she allowed herself to cook a little and then to sew again. She was still a successful lawyer, but her life took on a rounded shape. She laughed more, looked prettier. "I can't believe I am doing this!" she would announce with delight as she launched into some new venture. And then, "I can't believe I didn't do this sooner!"

By holding lightly to an attitude of gentle exploration, we can begin to lean into creative expansion. By replacing "No way!" with "Maybe," we open the door to mystery and to magic.

This newly positive attitude is the beginning of trust. We

are starting to look for the silver lining in what appears to be adversity. Most of us find that as we work with the morning pages, we begin to treat ourselves more gently. Feeling less desperate, we are less harsh with ourselves and with others. This compassion is one of the first fruits of aligning our creativity with its creator.

As we come to trust and love our internal guide, we lose our fear of intimacy because we no longer confuse our intimate others with the higher power we are coming to know. In short, we are learning to give up idolatry—the worshipful dependency on any person, place, or thing. Instead, we place our dependency on the source itself. The source meets our needs through people, places, and things.

This concept is a very hard one for most of us to really credit. We tend to believe we must go out and shake a few trees to make things happen. I would not deny that shaking a few trees is good for us. In fact, I believe it is necessary. I call it *doing the footwork*. I want to say, however, that while the footwork is necessary, I have seldom seen it pay off in a linear fashion. It seems to work more like we shake the apple tree and the universe delivers oranges.

Time and again, I have seen a recovering creative do the footwork of becoming internally clear and focused about dreams and delights, take a few outward steps in the direction of the dream—only to have the universe fling open an unsuspected door. One of the central tasks of creative recovery is learning to accept this generosity.

THE VIRTUE TRAP

An artist must have downtime, time to do nothing. Defending our right to such time takes courage, conviction, and resiliency. Such time, space, and quiet will strike our family and friends as a withdrawal from them. It is.

For an artist, withdrawal is necessary. Without it, the artist in us feels vexed, angry, out of sorts. If such deprivation continues, our artist becomes sullen, depressed, hostile. We eventually became like cornered animals, snarling at our family

Often people attempt to live their lives backwards: they try to have more things, or more money, in order to do more of what they want so that they will be happier. The way it actually works is the reverse. You must first be *who you really are, then,* do *what you need to do, in order to* have *what you want.*

MARGARET YOUNG

and friends to leave us alone and stop making unreasonable demands.

We are the ones making unreasonable demands. We expect
our artist to be able to function without giving it what it needs
to do so. An artist requires the upkeep of creative solitude. An
artist requires the healing of time alone. Without this period of
recharging, our artist becomes depleted. Over time, it becomes something worse than out of sorts. Death threats are
issued.

In the early stages, these death threats are issued to our intimates. ("I could kill you when you interrupt me. . . . ") Woe
to the spouse who doesn't take the hint. Woe to the hapless
child who doesn't give you solitude. ("You're making me very
angry. . . . ")

Over time, if our warnings are ignored and we deem to
stay in whatever circumstance—marriage, job, friendship—
requires threats and warnings, homicide gives way to suicide.
"I want to kill myself" replaces "I could murder you."

"What's the use?" replaces our feelings of joy and satisfaction. We may go through the actions of continuing our life. We
may even continue to produce creatively, but we are leaching
blood from ourselves, vampirizing our souls. In short, we are
on the treadmill of virtuous production and we are caught.

We are caught in the virtue trap.

There are powerful payoffs to be found in staying stuck
and deferring nurturing your sense of self. For many creatives,
the belief that they must be nice and worry about what will
happen with their friends, family, mate if they dare to do what
they really want to constitutes a powerful reason for non-
action.

A man who works in a busy office may crave and need the
retreat of solitude. Nothing would serve him better than a vacation alone, but he thinks that's selfish so he doesn't do it. It
wouldn't be nice to his wife.

A woman with two small children wants to take a pottery
class. It conflicts with some of her son's Little League practices,
and she wouldn't be able to attend as faithful audience. She cancels pottery and plays the good mother—seething on the sidelines with resentments.

*We are traditionally rather proud
of ourselves for having slipped
creative work in their between the
domestic chores and obligations.
I'm not sure we deserve such big
A-pluses for that.*

TONI MORRISON

You build up a head of steam. If you're four days out of the studio, on the fifth day you really crash in there. You will kill anybody who disturbs you on that fifth day, when you desperately need it.

SUSAN ROTHENBERG

A young father with a serious interest in photography, yearns for a place in the home to pursue his interest. The installation of a modest family darkroom would require dipping into savings and deferring the purchase of a new couch. The darkroom doesn't get set up but the new couch does.

Many recovering creatives sabotage themselves most frequently by making nice. There is a tremendous cost to such ersatz virtue.

Many of us have made a virtue out of deprivation. We have embraced a long-suffering artistic anorexia as a martyr's cross. We have used it to feed a false sense of spirituality grounded in being good, meaning *superior.*

I call this seductive, faux spirituality the Virtue Trap. Spirituality has often been misused as a route to an unloving solitude, a stance where we proclaim ourselves above our human nature. This spiritual superiority is really only one more form of denial. For an artist, virtue can be deadly. The urge toward respectability and maturity can be stultifying, even fatal.

We strive to be good, to be nice, to be helpful, to be unselfish. We want to be generous, of service, of the world. *But what we really want is to be left alone.* When we can't get others to leave us alone, we eventually abandon ourselves. To others, we may look like we're there. We may act like we're there. But our true self has gone to ground.

What's left is a shell of our whole self. It stays because it is caught. Like a listless circus animal prodded into performing, it does its tricks. It goes through its routine. It earns its applause. But all of the hoopla falls on deaf ears. We are dead to it. Our artist is not merely out of sorts. Our artist has checked out. Our life is now an out-of-body experience. We're gone. A clinician might call it disassociating. I call it leaving the scene of the crime.

"Come out, come out, wherever you are," we wheedle, but our creative self no longer trusts us. Why should it? We sold it out.

Afraid to appear selfish, we lose our self. We become self-destructive. Because this self-murder is something we seek passively rather than consciously act out, we are often blind to its poisonous grip on us.

The question "Are you self-destructive?" is asked so frequently that we seldom hear it accurately. What it means is *Are you destructive of your self?* And what that really asks us is *Are you destructive of your true nature?*

Many people, caught in the virtue trap, do not appear to be self-destructive to the casual eye. Bent on being good husbands, fathers, mothers, wives, teachers, whatevers, they have constructed a false self that looks good to the world and meets with a lot of worldly approval. This false self is always patient, always willing to defer its needs to meet the needs or demands of another. ("What a great guy! That Fred gave up his concert tickets to help me move on a Friday night. . . .")

Virtuous to a fault, these trapped creatives have destroyed the true self, the self that didn't meet with much approval as a child. The self who heard repeatedly, "Don't be selfish!" The true self is a disturbing character, healthy and occasionally anarchistic, who knows how to play, how to say no to others and "yes" to itself.

Creatives who are caught in the Virtue Trap still cannot let themselves approve of this true self. They can't show it to the world without dreading the world's continued disapproval. ("Can you believe it? Fred used to be such a nice guy. Always ready to help me out. Anytime, anyplace. I asked him to help me move last week and he said he was going to a play. When did Fred get so cultured, I ask you?")

Fred knows full well that if he stops being so nice, Fabulous Fred, his outsized, nice-guy alter ego, will bite the dust. Martyred Mary knows the same thing as she agrees to round five of baby-sitting for her sister so *she* can go out. Saying no to her sister would be saying yes to herself, and that is a responsibility that Mary just can't handle. Free on a Friday night? What would she do with herself? That's a good question, and one of many that Mary and Fred use their virtue to ignore.

"Are you self-destructive?" is a question that the apparently virtuous would be bound to answer with a resounding no. They then conjure up a list proving how responsible they are. But responsible to whom? The question is "*Are* you self-destructive?" Not "Do you *appear* self-destructive?" And most definitely not "Are you nice to other people?"

Nobody objects to a woman being a good writer or sculptor or geneticist if at the same time she manages to be a good wife, good mother, good-looking, good-tempered, well-groomed, and unaggressive.

LESLIE M. MCINTYRE

We listen to other people's ideas of what is self-destructive without ever looking at whether their self and our self have similar needs. Caught in the Virtue Trap, we refuse to ask ourselves, "What are my needs? What would I do if it weren't too selfish?"

Are you self-destructive?

This is a very difficult question to answer. To begin with, it requires that we know something of our true self (and that is the very self we have been systematically destroying).

One quick way to ascertain the degree of drift is to ask yourself this question: what would I try if it weren't too crazy?

1. Sky diving, scuba diving.

2. Belly dancing, Latin dancing.

3. Getting my poems published.

4. Buying a drum set.

5. Bicycling through France.

If your list looks pretty exciting, even if crazy, then you are on the right track. These crazy notions are actually voices from our true self. What would I do if it weren't too selfish?

1. Sign up for scuba lessons.

2. Take the Latin dancing class at the Y.

3. Buy *The Poet's Market* and make a submission a week.

4. Get the used drum set my cousin is trying to sell.

5. Call my travel agent and check out France.

By seeking the creator within and embracing our own gift of creativity, we learn to be spiritual in this world, to trust that God is good and so are we and so is all of creation. In this way, we avoid the Virtue Trap.

There is the risk you cannot afford to take, [and] there is the risk you cannot afford not to take.

PETER DRUCKER

THE VIRTUE-TRAP QUIZ

1. The biggest lack in my life is _____.

2. The greatest joy in my life is _____.

3. My largest time commitment is _____.

4. As I play more, I work _____.

5. I feel guilty that I am _____.

6. I worry that _____.

7. If my dreams come true, my family will _____.

8. I sabotage myself so people will _____.

9. If I let myself feel it, I'm angry that I _____.

10. One reason I get sad sometimes is _____.

You will do foolish things, but do them with enthusiasm.

COLETTE

Does your life serve you or only others? Are you self-destructive?

FORBIDDEN JOYS, AN EXERCISE

One of the favored tricks of blocked creatives is saying no to ourselves. It is astonishing the number of small ways we discover to be mean and miserly with ourselves. When I say this to my students, they often protest that this is not true—that they are very good to themselves. Then I ask them to do this exercise.

List ten things you love and would love to do but are not allowed to do. Your list might look like this:

1. Go dancing.

2. Carry a sketch book.

3. Roller-skate.

4. Buy new cowboy boots.

5. Streak your hair blond.

6. Go on vacation.

7. Take flying lessons.

8. Move to a bigger place.

9. Direct a play.

10. Take life-drawing class.

Very often, the mere act of writing out your list of forbidden joys breaks down your barriers to doing them.

Post your list somewhere highly visible.

WISH LIST, AN EXERCISE

One of the best ways we can evade our Censor is to use the technique of speed writing. Because wishes are just wishes, they are allowed to be frivolous (and frequently should be taken very seriously). As quickly as you can, finish the following phrases.

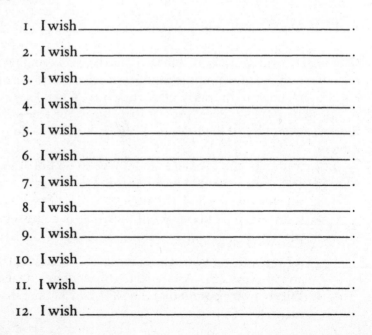

1. I wish _____ .

2. I wish _____ .

3. I wish _____ .

4. I wish _____ .

5. I wish _____ .

6. I wish _____ .

7. I wish _____ .

8. I wish _____ .

9. I wish _____ .

10. I wish _____ .

11. I wish _____ .

12. I wish _____ .

13. I wish _____ .

14. I wish _____ .

15. I wish _____ .

16. I wish _____ .

17. I wish _____ .

18. I wish _____ .

19. I most especially wish _____ .

The specific meaning of God depends on what is the most desirable good for a person.

ERICH FROMM

TASKS ✉

The following tasks explore and expand your relationship to the source.

1. The reason I can't really believe in a *supportive* God is . . . List five grievances. (God can take it.)

2. Starting an Image File: If I had either faith or money I would try . . . List five desires. For the next week, be alert for images of these desires. When you spot them, clip them, buy them, photograph them, draw them, *collect them somehow.* With these images, begin a file of dreams that speak to you. Add to it continually for the duration of the course.

3. One more time, list five imaginary lives. Have they changed? Are you doing more parts of them? You may want to add images of these lives to your image file.

4. If I were twenty and had money . . . List five adventures. Again, add images of these to your visual image file.

5. If I were sixty-five and had money . . . List five postponed pleasures. And again, collect these images. This is a very potent tool. I now live in a house that I *imaged* for ten years.

6. Ten ways I am mean to myself are . . . Just as making the positive explicit helps allow it into our lives, making the negative explicit helps us to exorcise it.

7. Ten items I would like to own that I don't are . . . And again, you may want to collect these images. In order to boost sales, experts in sales motivation often teach rookie salesmen to post images of what they would like to own. It works.

8. Honestly, my favorite creative block is . . . TV, overreading, friends, work, rescuing others, overexercise. You name it. Whether you can draw or not, please cartoon yourself indulging in it.

9. My payoff for staying blocked is . . . This you may want to explore in your morning pages.

10. The person I blame for being blocked is . . . Again, use your pages to mull on this.

CHECK-IN

1. How many days this week did you do your morning pages? Are you starting to like them—at all? How was the experience for you? Have you discovered the page-and-a-half *truth point* yet? Many of us find that pay dirt in our writing occurs after a page and a half of vamping.

2. Did you do your artist date this week? Have you had the experience of hearing answers during this leisure time? What did you do for your date? How did it feel? Have you taken an artist date yet that really felt adventurous?

3. Did you experience any synchronicity this week? What was it? Try inaugurating a conversation on synchronicity with your friends.

4. Were there any other issues this week that you consider significant for your recovery? Describe them.

Recovering a Sense of Abundance

This week you tackle a major creative block—money. You are asked to really look at your own ideas around God, money, and creative abundance. The essays will explore the ways in which your attitudes limit abundance and luxury in your current life. You will be introduced to counting, a block-busting tool for clarity and right use of funds. This week may feel volatile.

THE GREAT CREATOR

"I'm a believer," Nancy declares. "I just don't believe God gets involved with money." Although she doesn't recognize it, Nancy carries two self-sabotaging beliefs. She believes not only that God is good—too good to do money—but also that money is bad. Nancy, like many of us, needs to overhaul her God concept in order to fully recover her creativity.

For many of us, raised to believe that money is the real source of security, a dependence on God feels foolhardy, suicidal, even laughable. When we consider the lilies of the fields, we think they are quaint, too out of it for the modern world. We're the ones who keep clothes on our backs. We're the ones who buy the groceries. And we will pursue our art, we tell ourselves, when we have enough money to do it easily.

And when will that be?

We want a God that feels like a fat paycheck and a license to spend as we please. Listening to the siren song of *more,* we are deaf to the still small voice waiting in our soul to whisper, "You're enough."

"Seek ye first the kingdom of heaven and all things will be

Money is God in action.

RAYMOND CHARLES
BARKER

The more we learn to operate in the world based on trust in our intuition, the stronger our channel will be and the more money we will have.

SHAKTI GAWAIN

Money will come when you are doing the right thing.

MIKE PHILLIPS

added to it," we have been told, often since childhood, by people quoting from the Bible. We don't believe this. And we certainly don't believe it about art. Maybe God would feed and clothe us, in a pinch, but painting supplies? A museum tour of Europe, dance classes? God's not about to spring for those, we tell ourselves. We cling to our financial concerns as a way to avoid not only our art but also our spiritual growth. Our faith is in the dollar. "I have to keep a roof over my head," we say. "Nobody's going to pay me to be more creative."

We are awfully sure about that. Most of us harbor a secret belief that work has to be work and not play, and that anything we really want to do—like write, act, dance—must be considered frivolous and be placed a distant second. This is not true.

We are operating out of the toxic old idea that God's will for us and our will for us are at opposite ends of the table. "I want to be an actress, but God wants me to wait tables in hash joints," the scenario goes. "So if I try to be an actress, I will end up slinging hash."

Thinking like this is grounded in the idea that God is a stern parent with very rigid ideas about what's appropriate for us. And you'd better believe we won't like them. This stunted god concept needs alteration.

This week, in your morning pages, write about the god you do believe in and the god you would like to believe in. For some of us, this means, "What if God's a woman and she's on my side?" For others, it is a god of energy. For still others, a collective of higher forces moving us toward our highest good. If you are still dealing with a god consciousness that has remained unexamined since childhood, you are probably dealing with a toxic god. What would a nontoxic god think of your creative goals? Might such a god really exist? If so, would money or your job or your lover remain your higher power?

Many of us equate difficulty with virtue—and art with fooling around. Hard work is good. A terrible job must be building our moral fiber. Something—a talent for painting, say—that comes to us easily and seems compatible with us must be some sort of cheap trick, not to be taken seriously. On the one hand, we give lip service to the notion that God wants us to be happy, joyous, and free. On the other, we secretly think that God wants us to be broke if we are going to be so decadent as to want to be artists. Do we have any proof at all for these ideas about God?

Looking at God's creation, it is pretty clear that the creator itself did not know when to stop. There is not one pink flower, or even fifty pink flowers, but hundreds. Snowflakes, of course, are the ultimate exercise in sheer creative glee. No two alike. This creator looks suspiciously like someone who just might send us support for our creative ventures.

"We have a new employer," the Big Book of Alcoholics Anonymous promises recovering alcoholics. "If we take care of God's business he will take care of ours." To battered AA newcomers, such thinking is a lifeline. Desperate for a way to achieve sobriety, they cling to this thought when worried about their own precarious abilities to live effectively. Expecting divine help, they tend to receive it. Tangled lives smooth out; tangled relationships gain sanity and sweetness.

To those less desperate, such assurances sound foolish, even deceptive, like we're being conned. The God who has a job for us? The God who has fulfilling work? The God who holds abundance and dignity, who holds a million possibilities, the keys to every door? This God can sound suspiciously like a flimflam man.

And so, when it comes time for us to choose between a cherished dream and a lousy current drudgery, we often choose to ignore the dream and blame our continued misery on God. We act like it's God's fault we didn't go to Europe, take that painting class, go on that photo shoot. In truth, we, not God, have decided not to go. We have tried to be sensible—as though we have any proof at all that God is sensible—rather than see if the universe might not have supported some healthy extravagance.

The creator may be our father/mother/source but it is surely not the father/mother/church/teacher/friends here on earth who have instilled in us their ideas of what is sensible for us. Creativity is not and never has been sensible. Why should it be? Why should you be? Do you still think there is some moral

Always leave enough time in your life to do something that makes you happy, satisfied, even joyous. That has more of an effect on economic well-being than any other single factor.

PAUL HAWKEN

virtue in being martyred? If you want to make some art, make some art. Just a little art . . . two sentences. One rhyme. A silly kindergarten ditty:

> *God likes art.*
> *That's the part*
> *My parents would ignore.*
> *God likes art,*
> *And I make art.*
> *That's what God likes me for!*

All substance is energy in motion. It lives and flows. Money is symbolically a golden, flowing stream of concretized vital energy.

THE MAGICAL WORK
OF THE SOUL

Making art begins with making hay while the sun shines. It begins with getting into the *now* and enjoying your day. It begins with giving yourself some small treats and breaks. "This is extravagant but so is God" is a good attitude to take when treating your artist to small bribes and beauties. Remember, you are the cheapskate, not God. As you expect God to be more generous, God will be able to be more generous to you.

What we really want to do is what we are really meant to do. When we do what we are meant to do, money comes to us, doors open for us, we feel useful, and the work we do feels like play to us.

We will continue to work this week with our ideas surrounding money. We will see how our ideas about money ("It's hard to get. You have to work long hours for it. You need to worry about money first and creativity second") shape our ideas about creativity.

LUXURY

For those of us who have become artistically anorectic— yearning to be creative and refusing to feed that hunger in ourselves so that we become more and more focused on our deprivation—a little authentic luxury can go a long way. The key work here is *authentic*. Because art is born in expansion, in a belief in sufficient supply, it is critical that we pamper ourselves for the sense of abundance it brings to us.

What constitutes pampering? That will vary for each of us. For Gillian, a pair of new-to-her tweed trousers from the vintage store conjured up images of Carole Lombard laughter and racy roadsters. For Jean, a single, sprightly Gerber daisy perched on her night table told her life was abloom with possibility. Matthew found that the scent of real furniture wax gave him a feeling of safety, solidity, and order. Constance found luxury in allowing herself the indulgence of a magazine subscription (a twenty-dollar gift that keeps giving for a full year of images and indulgence).

All too often, we become blocked and blame it on our lack of money. This is *never* an authentic block. The actual block is our feeling of constriction, our sense of powerlessness. Art requires us to empower ourselves with choice. At the most basic level, this means choosing to do self-care.

One of my friends is a world-famous artist of formidable talents. He is assured a place in history for his contributions to his field. He is sought after by younger artists and respected by older artists. Although not yet fifty, he has already been singled out for lifetime achievement awards. Nonetheless, this is an artist suffering in the throes of artistic anorexia. Although he continues to work, he does so at greater and greater cost to himself. Why, he sometimes wonders to himself, does his life's work now feel so much like his life's *work*?

Why? Because he has denied himself luxury.

Let me be clear that the luxury I am talking about here has nothing to do with penthouse views, designer clothes, zippy foreign sports cars, or first-class travel. This man enjoys all those privileges, but what he doesn't enjoy is his life. He has denied himself the luxury of time: time with friends, time with family, above all, time to himself with no agendas of preternatural accomplishment. His many former passions have dwindled to mere interests; he is too busy to enjoy pastimes. He tells himself he has no time to pass. The clock is ticking and he is using it to get famous.

Recently, I bought myself a horse for the first time in a decade. On hearing the good news, my accomplished friend moved immediately into his Wet Blanket mode, cautioning, "Well, I hope you don't expect to get to ride it much or even see it much. As you get older, you do less and less of the things you enjoy. Life becomes more and more about doing what you must. . . ."

Because I have learned to hear Wet Blanket messages for what they are, I was not too daunted by this prognosis. But I was saddened by it. It reminded me of the vulnerability of all artists, even very famous ones, to the shaming, "I should be working" side of themselves that discourages creative pleasures.

In order to thrive as artists—and, one could argue, as people—we need to be available to the universal flow. When we put a stopper on our capacity for joy by anorectically declining the small gifts of life, we turn aside the larger gifts as well. Those of us, like my artist friend, who are engaged in long creative works will find ourselves leaching our souls to find images, returning to past work, to tricks, practicing our craft more than enlarging our art. Those of us who have stymied the work flow completely will find ourselves in lives that feel barren and devoid of interest no matter how many meaningless things we have filled them with.

What gives us true joy? That is the question to ask concerning luxury, and for each of us the answer is very different. For Berenice, the answer is raspberries, fresh raspberries. She laughs at how easily pleased she is. For the cost of a pint of raspberries, she buys herself an experience of abundance. Sprinkled on cereal, cut up with a peach, poured over a scoop of ice cream. She can buy her abundance at the supermarket and even get it quick frozen if she has to.

"They cost $1.98 to $4.50, depending on the season. I always tell myself they are too expensive, but the truth is that's a bargain for a week of luxury. It's less than a movie. Less than a deluxe cheeseburger. I guess it's just more than I thought I was worth."

For Alan, music is the great luxury. A musician when he was younger, he had long denied himself the right to play. Like most blocked creatives, he suffered from a deadly duo: artistic anorexia and prideful perfectionism. There were no practice shots for this player. He wanted to be at the top, and if he couldn't be there he wouldn't be anywhere near his beloved music.

I'd rather have roses on my table than diamonds on my neck.

EMMA GOLDMAN

Stuck and stymied, Alan described his block this way: "I try to play and I hear myself, and what I can do is so far away from what I want to do that I cringe." (And then quit.)

Working on his creative recovery, Alan began by allowing himself the luxury of buying a new recording a week. He stopped making music work and started making it fun again. He was to buy crazy recordings, not just high art. Forget high-minded aspirations. What sounded like fun?

Explore daily the will of God.

C. G. JUNG

Alan began exploring. He bought gospel, country and western, Indian drum music. A month of this and he impulsively bought a set of practice sticks at the music store. He let them lie and let them lie and . . .

Three months later, Alan was drumming on the handle-bars of his exercise bike while rock and roll blasted through his Walkman. Two months later, he cleared a space in the attic and acquired a secondhand drum kit.

"I thought my wife and daughter would be embarrassed by how bad I was," he explains. Catching himself in his blaming, he cops, "Actually, I was the one who was embarrassed, but now I'm just having fun with it and actually sounding a little better to myself. For an old guy, I'd say my chops are coming back."

For Laura, a dime-store set of watercolor paints was her first foray into luxury. For Kathy, it was a deluxe Crayola set, "the kind my mother would never get me. I let myself do two drawings the first night, and one of them was a sketch of me in my new life, the one I am working toward."

But for many blocked creatives, it takes a little work to even *imagine* ourselves having luxury. Luxury is a learned practice for most of us. Blocked creatives are often the Cinderellas of the world. Focused on others at the expense of ourselves, we may even be threatened by the idea of spoiling ourselves for once.

"Don't try to let go of Cinderella," my writer friend Karen advises. "Keep Cinderella but focus on giving yourself the glass slipper. The second half of that fairy tale is great."

What we are talking about when we discuss luxury is very often a shift in consciousness more than flow—although as we acknowledge and invite what feels luxurious to us, we may indeed trigger an increased flow.

Creative living requires the luxury of time, which we carve out for ourselves—even if it's fifteen minutes for quick morning pages and a ten-minute minibath after work.

Creative living requires the luxury of space for ourselves, even if all we manage to carve out is one special bookshelf and a windowsill that is ours. (My study has a window shelf of paperweights and seashells.) Remember that your artist is a youngster and youngsters like things that are "mine." My chair. My book. My pillow.

Designating a few things special and yours alone can go a long way toward making you feel pampered. Chinatown anywhere offers a beautiful teacup and saucer for under five dollars. Secondhand stores often have one-of-a-kind china plates that make an afternoon snack a more creative experience.

Much of what we do in a creative recovery may seem silly. Silly is a defense our Wet Blanket adult uses to squelch our artist child. Beware of *silly* as a word you toss at yourself. Yes, artist dates *are* silly—that's the whole point.

Creativity lives in paradox: serious art is born from serious play.

True life is lived when tiny changes occur.

LEO TOLSTOY

COUNTING, AN EXERCISE

For the next week you will be discovering how you spend your money. Buy a small pocket notepad and write down every nickel you spend. It doesn't matter what it is for, how tiny the purchase, how petty the amount. Petty cash is still cash.

Each day, date a page and count—what you bought, what you spent, where your money went, whether it was for groceries, lunch in a diner, a cab ride, subway fares, or a loan to your brother. Be meticulous. Be thorough. And be nonjudgmental. This is an exercise in self-observation—*not* self-flagellation.

You may want to continue this practice for a full month or longer. It will teach you what you value in terms of your spending. Often our spending differs from our real values. We fritter away cash on things we don't cherish and deny ourselves those things we do. For many of us, counting is a necessary prelude to learning creative luxury.

MONEY MADNESS, AN EXERCISE

Complete the following phrases.

1. People with money are _____.
2. Money makes people _____.
3. I'd have more money if _____.
4. My dad thought money was _____.
5. My mom always thought money would _____.
6. In my family, money caused _____.
7. Money equals _____.
8. If I had money, I'd _____.
9. If I could afford it, I'd _____.
10. If I had some money, I'd _____.
11. I'm afraid that if I had money I would _____.
12. Money is _____.
13. Money causes _____.
14. Having money is not _____.
15. In order to have more money, I'd need to _____.
16. When I have money, I usually _____.
17. I think money _____.
18. If I weren't so cheap I'd _____.
19. People think money _____.
20. Being broke tells me _____.

TASKS ✉

1. Natural Abundance: Find five pretty or interesting rocks. I enjoy this exercise particularly because rocks

can be carried in pockets, fingered in business meetings. They can be small, constant reminders of our creative consciousness.

As an artist, it is central to be unsatisfied! This isn't greed, though it might be appetite.

LAWRENCE CALCAGNO

2. Natural Abundance: Pick five flowers or leaves. You may want to press these between wax paper and save them in a book. If you did this in kindergarten, that's fine. Some of the best creative play is done there. Let yourself do it again.

3. Clearing: Throw out or give away five ratty pieces of clothing.

4. Creation: Bake something. (If you have a sugar problem, make a fruit salad.) Creativity does not have to always involve capital-*A* art. Very often, the act of cooking something can help you cook something up in another creative mode. When I am stymied as a writer, I make soups and pies.

5. Communication: Send postcards to five friends. This is not a goody-two-shoes exercise. Send to people you would *love* to hear from.

7. Reread the Basic Principles. (See page 3.) Do this once daily. Read an Artist's Prayer—yours from Week Four or mine on pages 207–208. Do this once daily.

8. Clearing: Any new changes in your home environment? Make some.

9. Acceptance: Any new flow in your life? Practice saying yes to freebies.

10. Prosperity: Any changes in your financial situation or your perspective on it? Any new—even crazy— ideas about what you would love doing? Pull images around this and add to your image file.

CHECK-IN 🖉

1. How many days this week did you do your morning pages? (Have you used them yet to think about cre-

ative luxury for yourself?) How was the experience for you?

2. Did you do your artist date this week? (Have you considered allowing yourself two?) What did you do? How did it feel?

3. Did you experience any synchronicity this week? What was it?

4. Were there any other issues this week that you consider significant for your recovery? Describe them.

Recovering a Sense of Connection

We turn this week to the practice of right attitudes for creativity. The emphasis is on your receptive as well as active skills. The essays, exercises, and tasks aim at excavating areas of genuine creative interest as you connect with your personal dreams.

LISTENING

The ability to listen is a skill we are honing with both our morning pages and our artist dates. The pages train us to hear past our Censor. The artist dates help us to pick up the voice of inspiration. While both of these activities are apparently unconnected to the actual act of making art, they are critical to the creative process.

Art is not about thinking something up. It is about the opposite—getting something down. The directions are important here.

If we are trying to *think something up*, we are straining to reach for something that's just beyond our grasp, "up there, in the stratosphere, where art lives on high. . . ."

When we *get something down*, there is no strain. We're not doing; we're getting. Someone or something else is doing the doing. Instead of reaching for inventions, we are engaged in listening.

When an actor is in the moment, he or she is engaged in listening for the next right thing creatively. When a painter is painting, he or she may begin with a plan, but that plan is soon

In the esoteric Judaism of the Cabalah, the Deep Self is named the Neshamah, from the root of Shmhm, "to hear or listen": the Neshamah is She Who Listens, the soul who inspires or guides us.

STARHAWK

surrendered to the painting's own plan. This is often expressed as "The brush takes the next stroke." In dance, in composition, in sculpture, the experience is the same: we are more the conduit than the creator of what we express.

Art is an act of tuning in and dropping down the well. It is as though all the stories, painting, music, performances in the world live just under the surface of our normal consciousness. Like an underground river, they flow through us as a stream of ideas that we can tap down into. As artists, we drop down the well into the stream. We hear what's down there and we act on it—more like taking dictation than anything fancy having to do with art.

A friend of mine is a superb film director who is known for his meticulous planning. And yet he often shoots most brilliantly from the seat of his pants, quickly grabbing a shot that comes to him as he works.

These moments of clear inspiration require that we move into them on faith. We can practice these small leaps of faith daily in our pages and on our artist dates. We can learn not only to listen but also to hear with increasing accuracy that inspired, intuitive voice that says, "Do this, try this, say this. . . ."

Most writers have had the experience of catching a poem or a paragraph or two of formed writing. We consider these finds to be small miracles. What we fail to realize is that they are, in fact, the norm. We are the instrument more than the author of our work.

Michelangelo is said to have remarked that he released David from the marble block he found him in. "The painting has a life of its own. I try to let it come through," said Jackson Pollock. When I teach screenwriting, I remind my students that their movie already exists in its entirety. Their job is to listen for it, watch it with their mind's eye, and write it down.

The same may be said of all art. If painting and sculptures wait for us, then sonatas wait for us; books, plays, and poems wait for us, too. Our job is simply to get them down. To do that, we drop down the well.

Some people find it easier to picture the stream of inspiration as being like radio waves of all sorts being broadcast at all times.

With practice, we learn how to hear the desired frequency on request. We tune in to the frequency we want. Like a parent, we learn to hear the voice of our current brainchild among the other children's voices.

Once you accept that it is natural to create, you can begin to accept a second idea—that the creator will hand you whatever you need for the project. The minute you are willing to accept the help of this collaborator, you will see useful bits of help everywhere in your life. Be alert: there is a second voice, a higher harmonic, adding to and augmenting your inner creative voice. This voice frequently shows itself in synchronicity.

Listening is a form of accepting.

STELLA TERRILL MANN

You will hear the dialogue you need, find the right song for the sequence, see the exact paint color you almost had in mind, and so forth. You will have the experience of finding things— books, seminars, tossed-out stuff—that happen to fit with what you are doing.

Learn to accept the possibility that the universe is helping you with what you are doing. Become willing to see the hand of God and accept it as a friend's offer to help with what you are doing. Because many of us unconsciously harbor the fearful belief that God would find our creations decadent or frivolous or worse, we tend to discount this creator-to-creator help.

Try to remember that God is the Great Artist. Artists like other artists.

Expect the universe to support your dream. It will.

PERFECTIONISM

Tillie Olsen correctly calls it the "knife of the perfectionist attitude in art." You may call it something else. *Getting it right,* you may call it, or *fixing it before I go any further.* You may call it *having standards.* What you should be calling it is *perfectionism.*

Perfectionism has nothing to do with getting it right. It has nothing to do with fixing things. It has nothing to do with standards. Perfectionism is a refusal to let yourself move ahead. It is a loop—an obsessive, debilitating closed system that causes you to get stuck in the details of what you are writing or painting or making and to lose sight of the whole.

Instead of creating freely and allowing errors to reveal themselves later as insights, we often get mired in getting the details right. We correct our originality into a uniformity that lacks passion and spontaneity. "Do not fear mistakes," Miles Davis told us. "There are none."

The perfectionist fixes one line of a poem over and over—until no lines are right. The perfectionist redraws the chin line on a portrait until the paper tears. The perfectionist writes so many versions of scene one that she never gets to the rest of the play. The perfectionist writes, paints, creates with one eye on her audience. Instead of enjoying the process, the perfectionist is constantly grading the results.

Cerebration is the enemy of originality in art.

MARTIN RITT

The perfectionist has married the logic side of the brain. The critic reigns supreme in the perfectionist's creative household. A brilliant descriptive prose passage is critiqued with a white-glove approach: "*Mmm.* What about this comma? Is this how you spell . . . ?"

For the perfectionist, there are no first drafts, rough sketches, warm-up exercises. Every draft is meant to be final, perfect, set in stone.

Midway through a project, the perfectionist decides to read it all over, outline it, see where it's going.

And where is it going? Nowhere, very fast.

The perfectionist is never satisfied. The perfectionist never says, "This is pretty good. I think I'll just keep going."

To the perfectionist, there is always room for improvement. The perfectionist calls this humility. In reality, it is egotism. It is pride that makes us want to write a perfect script, paint a perfect painting, perform a perfect audition monologue.

Perfectionism is not a quest for the best. It is a pursuit of the worst in ourselves, the part that tells us that nothing we do will ever be good enough—that we should try again.

No. We should not.

"A painting is never finished. It simply stops in interesting places," said Paul Gardner. A book is never finished. But at a certain point you stop writing it and go on to the next thing. A film is never cut perfectly, but at a certain point you let go and call it done. That is a normal part of creativity—letting go. We always do the best that we can by the light we have to see by.

RISK

QUESTION: What would I do if I didn't have to do it perfectly?

ANSWER: A great deal more than I am.

We've all heard that the unexamined life is not worth living, but consider too that the unlived life is not worth examin-
ing. The success of a creative recovery hinges on our ability to
move out of the head and into action. This brings us squarely
to risk. Most of us are practiced at talking ourselves out of
risk. We are skilled speculators on the probable pain of self-
exposure.

"I'll look like an idiot," we say, conjuring images of our
first acting class, our first hobbled short story, our terrible
drawings. Part of the game here is lining up the masters and
measuring our baby steps against their perfected craft. We
don't compare our student films to George Lucas's student
films. Instead, we compare them to *Star Wars*.

We deny that in order to do something well we must first
be willing to do it badly. Instead, we opt for setting our limits
at the point where we feel assured of success. Living within
these bounds, we may feel stifled, smothered, despairing,
bored. But, yes, we do feel safe. And safety is a very expensive
illusion.

In order to risk, we must jettison our accepted limits. We
must break through "I can't because . . ." Because I am too
old, too broke, too shy, too proud? Self-defended? Timorous?

Usually, when we say we can't do something, what we
mean is that we won't do something unless we can guarantee
that we'll do it perfectly.

Working artists know the folly of this stance. There is a
common joke among directors: "Oh, yeah. I always know exactly how I should direct the picture—after I'm done directing it."

As blocked artists, we unrealistically expect and demand
success from ourselves and recognition of that success from
others. With that as an unspoken demand, a great many things
remain outside our sphere of possibility. As actors, we tend to
allow ourselves to be typecast rather than working to expand
our range. As singers, we stay married to our safe material. As

*Living is a form of not being sure,
not knowing what next or how.
The moment you know how, you
begin to die a little. The artist
never entirely knows. We guess.
We may be wrong, but we take
leap after leap in the dark.*

AGNES DE MILLE

songwriters, we try to repeat a formula hit. In this way, artists who do not appear blocked to the outside eye experience themselves as blocked internally, unable to take the risk of moving into new and more satisfying artistic territory.

Once we are willing to accept that anything worth doing might even be worth doing badly our options widen. "If I didn't have to do it perfectly, I would try . . ."

1. Stand-up comedy.

2. Modern dancing.

3. Whitewater rafting.

4. Archery.

5. Learning German.

6. Figure drawing.

7. Figure skating.

8. Being a platinum blond.

9. Puppeteering.

10. Trapeze.

11. Water ballet.

12. Polo.

13. Wearing red lipstick.

14. Taking a couture class.

15. Writing short stories.

16. Reading my poetry in public.

17. A spontaneous tropical vacation.

18. Learning to shoot video.

19. Learning to ride a bike.

20. Taking a watercolor class.

We cannot escape fear. We can only transform it into a companion that accompanies us on all our exciting adventures. . . . Take a risk a day—one small or bold stroke that will make you feel great once you have done it.

SUSAN JEFFERS

In the movie *Raging Bull,* boxer Jake La Motta's manager-brother explains to him why he should shed some weight and fight an unknown opponent. After an intricate spiel that leaves La Motta baffled, he concludes, "So do it. If you win, you win, and if you lose, you win."

It is always that way with taking risks.

To put it differently, very often a risk is worth taking simply for the sake of taking it. There is something enlivening about expanding our self-definition, and a risk does exactly that. Selecting a challenge and meeting it creates a sense of self-empowerment that becomes the ground for further successful challenges. Viewed this way, running a marathon increases your chances of writing a full-length play. Writing a full-length play gives you a leg up on a marathon.

Complete the following sentence. "If I didn't have to do it perfectly, I would try . . ."

There is no must in art because art is free.

WASSILY KANDINSKY

Shoot for the moon. Even if you miss it you will land among the stars.

LES BROWN

JEALOUSY

Jealousy, I've often heard, is a normal human emotion. When I hear that, I think, "Maybe your jealousy—not mine."

My jealously roars in the head, tightens the chest, massages my stomach lining with a cold fist as it searches out the best grip. I have long regarded jealousy as my greatest weakness. Only recently have I seen it for the tough-love friend that it is.

Jealousy is a map. Each of our jealousy maps differs. Each of us will probably be surprised by some of the things we discover on our own. I, for example, have never been eaten alive with resentment over the success of women novelists. But I took an unhealthy interest in the fortunes and misfortunes of women playwrights. I was their harshest critic, until I wrote my first play.

With that action, my jealousy vanished, replaced by a feeling of camaraderie. My jealousy had actually been a mask for my fear of doing something I really wanted to do but was not yet brave enough to take action toward.

Jealousy is always a mask for fear: fear that we aren't able to get what we want; frustration that somebody else seems to be getting what is rightfully ours even if we are too frightened to reach for it. At its root, jealousy is a stingy emotion. It doesn't allow for the abundance and multiplicity of the universe. Jealousy tells us there is room for only one—one poet, one painter, one whatever you dream of being.

The truth, revealed by action in the direction of our dreams, is that there is room for all of us. But jealousy produces tunnel vision. It narrows our ability to see things in perspective. It strips us of our ability to see other options. The biggest lie that jealousy tells us is that we have no choice but to be jealous. Perversely, jealousy strips us of our will to act when action holds the key to our freedom.

THE JEALOUSY MAP, AN EXERCISE

Your jealousy map will have three columns. In the first column, name those whom you are jealous of. Next to each name write why. Be as specific and accurate as you can. In the third column, list one action you can take to move toward creative risk and out of jealousy.

When jealousy bites, like a snakebite it requires an immediate antidote. On paper, make your jealousy map.

WHO	WHY	ACTION ANTIDOTE
My sister Libby	She has a real art studio	Fix spare room
My friend Ed	Writes good crime novels	Try writing one
Anne Sexton	Famous poet	Publish my long-hoarded poems

Even the biggest changes begin with small ones. Green is the color of jealousy, but it is also the color of hope. When you learn to harness its fierce energy on your own behalf, jealousy is part of the fuel toward a greener and more verdant future.

With courage you will dare to take risks, have the strength to be compassionate and the wisdom to be humble. Courage is the foundation of integrity.

KESHAVAN NAIR

ARCHEOLOGY, AN EXERCISE

The phrases that follow are more of your sleuth work. Very often, we have buried parts of ourselves that can be uncovered by some digging. Not only will your answers tell you what you missed in the past; they will tell you what you can be doing, now, to comfort and encourage your artist child. It is not too late, no matter what your ego tells you.

I don't have a lot of respect for talent. Talent is genetic. It's what you do with it that counts.

MARTIN RITT

Complete these phrases.

1. As a kid, I missed the chance to _____.

2. As a kid, I lacked _____.

3. As a kid, I could have used _____.

4. As a kid, I dreamed of being _____.

5. As a kid, I wanted a _____.

6. In my house, we never had enough _____.

7. As a kid, I needed more _____.

8. I am sorry that I will never again see _____.

9. For years, I have missed and wondered about _____.

10. I beat myself up about the loss of _____.

It is important to acknowledge our positive inventory as well as our shortfalls. Take positive stock of what good you have to build on in the present.
Finish these phrases.

1. I have a loyal friend in _____.

2. One thing I like about my town is _____.

3. I think I have nice _____.

4. Writing my morning pages has shown me I can _____.

5. I am taking a greater interest in _____.

6. I believe I am getting better at _____.

7. My artist has started to pay more attention to _____.

8. My self-care is _____.

9. I feel more _____.

10. Possibly, my creativity is _____.

*Trust in yourself. Your percep-
tions are often far more accurate
than you are willing to believe.*

CLAUDIA BLACK

TASKS ✉

1. Make this phrase a mantra: *Treating myself like a precious object will make me strong.* Watercolor or crayon or
   calligraph this phrase. Post it where you will see it
   daily. We tend to think being hard on ourselves will
   make us strong. But it is cherishing ourselves that
   gives us strength.

2. Give yourself time out to listen to one side of an al-
   bum, just for joy. You may want to doodle as you listen, allowing yourself to draw the shapes, emotions,
   thoughts you hear in the music. Notice how just
   twenty minutes can refresh you. Learn to take these
   mini–artist dates to break stress and allow insight.

3. Take yourself into a sacred space—a church, synagogue, library, grove of trees—and allow yourself
   to savor the silence and healing solitude. Each of us
   has a personal idea of what sacred space is. For me, a
   large clock store or a great aquarium store can en-
   gender a sense of timeless wonder. Experiment.

4. Create one wonderful smell in your house—with
   soup, incense, fir branches, candles—whatever.

5. Wear your favorite item of clothing for no special oc-
   casion.

6. Buy yourself one wonderful pair of socks, one wonderful pair of gloves—one wonderfully comforting,
   self-loving something.

7. Collage: Collect a stack of at least ten magazines, which you will allow yourself to freely dismember. Setting a twenty-minute time limit for yourself, tear (literally) through the magazines, collecting any images that reflect your life or interests. Think of this collage as a form of pictorial autobiography. Include your past, present, future, and your dreams. It is okay to include images you simply like. Keep pulling until you have a good stack of images (at least twenty). Now take a sheet of newspaper, a stapler, or some tape or glue, and arrange your images in a way that pleases you. (This is one of my students' favorite exercises.)

8. Quickly list five favorite films. Do you see any common denominators among them? Are they romances, adventures, period pieces, political dramas, family epics, thrillers? Do you see traces of your cinematic themes in your collage?

9. Name your favorite topics to read about: comparative religion, movies, ESP, physics, rags-to-riches, betrayal, love triangles, scientific breakthroughs, sports . . . Are these topics in your collage?

10. Give your collage a place of honor. Even a secret place of honor is all right—in your closet, in a drawer, anywhere that is yours. You may want to do a new one every few months, or collage more thoroughly a dream you are trying to accomplish.

When you start a painting, it is somewhat outside you. At the conclusion, you seem to move inside the painting.

FERNANDO BOTERO

When an inner situation is not made conscious, it appears outside as fate.

C. G. JUNG

CHECK-IN ✐

1. How many days this week did you do your morning pages? Have you allowed yourself to daydream a few creative risks? Are you coddling your artist child with childhood loves?

2. Did you do your artist date this week? Did you use it to take any risks? What did you do? How did it feel?

3. Did you experience any synchronicity this week? What was it?

4. Were there any other issues this week that you consider significant for your recovery? Describe them.

Recovering a Sense of Strength

*T*his week tackles another major creative block: time. You will explore the ways in which you have used your perception of time to preclude taking creative risks. You will identify immediate and practical changes you can make in your current life. You will excavate the early conditioning that may have encouraged you to settle for far less than you desire creatively.

SURVIVAL

ONE OF THE MOST difficult tasks an artist must face is a primal one: artistic survival. All artists must learn the art of surviving loss: loss of hope, loss of face, loss of money, loss of self-belief. In addition to our many gains, we inevitably suffer these losses in an artistic career. They are the hazards of the road and, in many ways, its signposts. Artistic losses can be turned into artistic gains and strengths—but not in the isolation of the beleaguered artist's brain.

As mental-health experts are quick to point out, in order to move through loss and beyond it, we must acknowledge it and share it. Because artistic losses are seldom openly acknowledged or mourned, they become artistic scar tissue that blocks artistic growth. Deemed too painful, too silly, too humiliating to share and so to heal, they become, instead, secret losses.

If artistic creations are our brainchildren, artistic losses are our miscarriages. Women often suffer terribly, and privately, from losing a child who doesn't come to term. And as artists we suffer terrible losses when the book doesn't sell, the film doesn't get picked up, the juried show doesn't take our paintings, the best pot shatters, the poems are not accepted, the ankle injury sidelines us for an entire dance season.

We must remember that our artist is a child and that what we can handle intellectually far outstrips what we can handle emotionally. We must be alert to flag and mourn our losses.

The disappointing reception of a good piece of work, the inability to move across into a different medium or type of role due to other people's expectations of us are artistic losses that must be mourned. It does no good to say, "Oh, it happens to everybody" or "Who was I kidding anyway?" The unmourned disappointment becomes the barrier that separates us from future dreams. Not being cast in the role that's "yours," not being asked to join the company, having the show canceled or the play unreviewed—these are all losses.

Perhaps the most damaging form of artistic loss has to do with criticism. The artist within, like the child within, is seldom hurt by truth. I will say again that much true criticism liberates the artist it is aimed at. We are childlike, not childish. *Ah-hah!* is often the accompanying inner sound when a well-placed, accurate critical arrow makes its mark. The artist thinks, "Yes! I can see that! That's right! I can change that!"

The criticism that damages an artist is the criticism—well intentioned or ill—that contains no saving kernel of truth yet has a certain damning plausibility or an unassailable blanket judgment that cannot be rationally refuted.

Teachers, editors, mentors are often authority figures or parent figures for a young artist. There is a sacred trust inherent in the bond between teacher and student. This trust, when violated, has the impact of a parental violation. What we are talking about here is emotional incest.

A trusting student hears from an unscrupulous teacher that good work is bad or lacks promise or that he, the guru-teacher, senses a limit to the student's real talent or was mistaken in seeing talent, or doubts that there is talent. . . . Personal in nature, nebulous as to specifics, this criticism is like covert sexual harassment—a sullying yet hard to quantify experience. The student emerges shamed, feeling like a bad artist, or worse, a fool to try.

I shall become a master in this art only after a great deal of practice.

ERICH FROMM

Taking a new step, uttering a new word is what people fear most.

FYODOR DOSTOYEVSKI

THE IVORY POWER

It has been my perilous privilege over the past decade to under-take teaching forays into the groves of academia. It is my expe-rience as a visiting artist that many academics are themselves artistic beings who are deeply frustrated by their inability to create. Skilled in intellectual discourse, distanced by that intel-lectual skill from their own creative urgings, they often find the creativity of their charges deeply disturbing.

Imagination is more important than knowledge.

ALBERT EINSTEIN

Devoted as they are to the scholarly appreciation of art, most academics find the beast intimidating when viewed first-hand. Creative-writing programs tend to be regarded with jus-tified suspicion: those people aren't studying creativity, they're actually practicing it! Who knows where this could lead?

I am thinking particularly of a film-department chair of my acquaintance, a gifted filmmaker who for many years had been unable or unwilling to expose himself to the rigors and disappointments of creating. Channeling his ferocious cre-ative urges into the lives of his students, he alternately over-controlled and undercut their best endeavors, seeking to vicar-iously fulfill or justify his own position on the sidelines.

As much as I wanted to dislike this man—and I certainly disliked his behaviors—I found myself unable to regard him without compassion. His own thwarted creativity, so lumi-nous in his early films, had darkened to shadow first his own life and then the lives of his students. In the truest sense, he was a creative monster.

It took more years and more teaching for me to realize that academia harbors a far more subtle and deadly foe to the cre-ative spirit. Outright hostility, after all, can be encountered. Far more dangerous, far more soul-chilling, is the subtle dis-counting that may numb student creativity in the academic grove.

I am thinking now of my time at a distinguished research university, where my teaching colleagues published widely and well on film topics of the most esoteric and exotic stripe. Highly regarded among their intellectual peers, deeply im-mersed in their own academic careers, these colleagues offered scant mirroring to the creative students who passed through

*Surround yourself with people
who respect and treat you well.*

CLAUDIA BLACK

*To the rationally minded the
mental processes of the intuitive
appear to work backwards.*

FRANCES WICKES

their tutelage. They neglected to supply that most rudimentary nutrient: encouragement.

Creativity cannot be comfortably quantified in intellectual terms. By its very nature, creativity eschews such containment. In a university where the intellectual life is built upon the art of criticizing—on deconstructing a creative work—the art of creation itself, the art of creative construction, meets with scanty support, understanding, or approval. To be blunt, most academics know how to take something apart, but not how to assemble it.

Student work, when scrutinized, was seldom *appreciated.* Far from it. Whatever its genuine accomplishments, it was viewed solely in terms of its shortfalls. Time and again I saw promising work met with a volley of should-have-dones, could-have-dones, and might-have-dones, instead of being worked with as it was.

It is not my argument that the world of academia be turned into an exalted artists' studio. It is, however, my point that artists attempting to exist, grow, even flourish, within that milieu recognize that the entire thrust of intellectualism runs counter to the creative impulse. For an artist, to become overly cerebral is to become crippled. This is not to say that artists lack rigor; rather, that artistic rigor is grounded differently than intellectual life usually admits.

Artists and intellectuals are not the same animal. As a younger artist this was very confusing to me. I myself have considerable critical gifts, and have in fact won national awards for practicing them. It was to my own rue that I discovered that these same skills were misapplied when focused on embryonic artistic endeavors—mine or others. Younger artists are seedlings. Their early work resembles thicket and underbrush, even weeds. The halls of academia, with their preference for lofty intellectual theorems, do little to support the life of the forest floor. As a teacher, it has been my sad experience that many talented creatives were daunted early and unfairly by their inability to conform to a norm that was not their own. It would be my hope that the academics who read this book and apply it would do so with an altered appreciation for the authenticity of growth for the sake of growth. In other words, as taller trees, let us not allow our darker critical powers unfettered play upon the seedling artists in our midst.

Without specific tools and sufficient ego strengths, many gifted artists languish for years in the wake of such blows. Shamed at their supposed lack of talent, shamed by their "grandiose" dreams, the young artists may channel their gifts into commercial endeavors and then forget their dreams of doing more groundbreaking (and risky) work. They may work as editors instead of writers, film editors instead of film directors, commercial artists instead of fine artists, and get stuck within shouting distance of their dreams. Often audacity, not authentic talent, confers fame on an artist. The lack of audacity—pinched out by critical abuse or malnourished through neglect—may cripple many artists far superior to those we publicly acclaim. In order to recover our sense of hope and the courage to create, we must acknowledge and mourn the scars that are blocking us. This process may seem both painstaking and petty, but it is a necessary rite of passage. Just as a teenager must gain autonomy from an overbearing parent, so too an artist must gain autonomy from malignant artistic mentors.

Trust that still, small voice that says, "This might work and I'll try it."

DIANE MARIECHILD

When Ted finished writing his first novel, he bravely sent it off to a literary agent. He also sent a check for one hundred dollars to pay the agent for taking the time and trouble to read it. What came back was a single page of unusable, irresponsible, and vague reaction: "This novel is half good and half bad. That's the worst kind. I can't tell you how to fix it. I suggest pitching it out."

When I met Ted, he had been blocked for seven years. Like many beginners, he hadn't even known to get another opinion. It was with great difficulty that he handed his novel over to me. As Ted's friend, I was heartbroken for him that this novel had been manhandled. As a professional, I was impressed—so impressed I found myself with my first student to unblock.

"Please try to write again. You can do it. I know you can do it," I started in. Ted was willing to risk unblocking. It is now twelve years since Ted began his work with the morning pages. He has written three novels and two movies. He has an impressive literary agent and a growing reputation.

In order to get to where he is now, Ted had to refeel and mourn the wounding he had endured as a young writer. He had to make his peace with the lost years this wounding had cost him. A page at a time, a day at a time, he had to slowly build strength.

Like the career of any athlete, an artist's life will have its injuries. These go with the game. The trick is to survive them, to learn how to let yourself heal. Just as a player who ignores a sore muscle may tear it further, an artist who buries his pain over losses will ultimately cripple himself into silence. Give yourself the dignity of admitting your artistic wounds. That is the first step in healing them.

No inventory of our artistic injuries would be complete without acknowledging those wounds that are self-inflicted. Many times, as artists, we are offered a chance that we balk at, sabotaged by our fear, our low self-worth, or simply our other agendas.

Grace is offered an art scholarship in another city but doesn't want to leave Jerry, her boyfriend. She turns the scholarship down.

Jack is offered a dream job in his field in a faraway city. It's a great job but he turns it down because of all the friends and family he has where he is.

Angela gets terrible reviews in a terrible play and is then offered another lead in a challenging play. She turns it down.

These lost chances often haunt us bitterly in later years. We will work more extensively later with our artistic U-turns, but for now, just counting them as losses begins the process of healing them.

GAIN DISGUISED AS LOSS

Art is the act of structuring time. "Look at it this way," a piece of art says. "Here's how I see it." As my waggish friend the novelist Eve Babitz remarks, "It's all in the frame." This is particularly true when what we are dealing with is an artistic loss. Every loss must always be viewed as a potential gain; it's all in the framing.

Man can learn nothing except by going from the known to the unknown.

CLAUDE BERNARD

Every end is a beginning. We know that. But we tend to forget it as we move through grief. Struck by a loss, we focus, understandably, on what we leave behind, the lost dream of the work's successful fruition and its buoyant reception. We need to focus on what lies ahead. This can be tricky. We may not know what lies ahead. And, if the present hurts this badly, we tend to view the future as impending pain.

"Gain disguised as loss" is a potent artist's tool. To acquire it, simply, brutally, ask: "How can this loss serve me? Where does it point my work?" The answers will surprise and liberate you. The trick is to metabolize pain as energy. The key to doing that is to know, to trust, and to act as if a silver lining exists if you are only willing to look at the work differently or to walk through a different door, one that you may have balked at.

"In order to catch the ball, you have to want to catch the ball," the film director John Cassavetes once told a young director. Hearing this, I took it to mean, "Stop complaining about the lousy curves you get thrown and stretch, reach for what you *really* want." I have tried to follow this advice.

For years, I played studio roulette. Repeatedly, original scripts were bought and not made. Repeatedly, fine work languished on studio shelves, the victim of revolving studio doors. Go pictures became dead overnight, except in my filmmaker's heart— which was breaking.

"That's just the way it is," I was told repeatedly. "If you want to see your films made, you must first sell yourself as a writer and then *if* one of yours scripts is made and *if* that film is a hit and *if* the climate warms up a little, *then* you *might* get a shot at directing. . . ."

I listened to this conventional wisdom for a long time, racking up loss after loss, writing script after script. Finally, after one loss too many, I began to look for the other door, the one I had refused to walk through. I decided to catch the ball: I became an independent filmmaker.

I left Hollywood. I went to Chicago, bought a used camera and, using my *Miami Vice* writing money, shot my own feature, a romantic, forties-style comedy. It was in the can for

I cannot expect even my own art to provide all of the answers— only to hope it keeps asking the right questions.

GRACE HARTIGAN

$31,000 and it looked good. Then, incredibly, my sound tapes were stolen. I finished the film anyway, dubbing it in its entirety. (Yes, crazy, but so was Cassavetes, my role model.) The result won foreign distribution and fine reviews abroad. And I learned a lot.

Art is a technique of communication. The image is the most complete technique of all communication.

CLAUS OLDENBURG

Because I asked "How?" instead of "Why me?" I now have a modest first feature to my credit. It might have happened if I had not taken matters into my own hands, but it might not have, either. Since 1974, I have worked vigorously and exhaustively as a film writer. I have written—and sold—features, short films, documentaries, docudramas, teleplays, movies of the week, and that bastardized movie, the miniseries. I have directed one feature and a half dozen short films. Less visibly, I have labored as a script doctor, credited and not, for hire and for love.

To boot, I have written a hundred–plus film essays, film interviews, think pieces, trend pieces, aesthetics pieces, more— all as I toiled as a writer for such diverse publications as *Rolling Stone*, the *New York Times*, the *Village Voice*, *New York*, *New West*, the *Los Angeles Times*, the *Chicago Tribune*, and, most conspicuously, *American Film*, where I served as a contributing editor for many years. In short, you might say I have done my dharma to my favored art form.

Why all of this diverse, hydra–headed productivity? Because I love movies, love making them, and did not want my losses to take me down. I learned, when hit by loss, to ask the right question: "What next?" instead of "Why me?"

Whenever I am willing to ask "What is necessary next?" I have moved ahead. Whenever I have taken no for a final answer I have stalled and gotten stuck. I have learned that the key to career resiliency is self-empowerment and choice.

If you look at long and successful creative careers, you will see this principle in action. The distinguished videographer Shirley Clarke began her creative career as a dancer. She first became a filmmaker so that there would be some properly made dance films. Distinguishing herself next as a first-rate feature director, winning renown in Europe if not directing jobs in American studios, Clarke became the first American director to shoot a feature in Harlem, the first American director to explore the range of hand-held camera, the American director that John Cassavetes, Martin Scorsese, and Paul Shrader all credit as seminal in their own artistic formation. Alas, she was a woman and she lived in difficult times. When her filmmaking revenues dried up, she became one of the first video artists, working with Sam Shepard, Joseph Papp, Ornette Coleman. Clarke clearly took to heart the idea that it was harder to hit a moving target. Whenever one avenue for her creativity was blocked, she found another.

The world of reality has its limits; the world of imagination is boundless.

JEAN-JACQUES
ROUSSEAU

Film annals abound with such stories. Elia Kazan, out of favor as a director, wrote novels. The director John Cassavetes, also a fine actor, used his acting to fund his directing efforts, which were too eclectic for studio backing. "If they won't make it as a feature, *I'll* make it," Cassavetes said, and he did. Rather than allow himself to be blocked, he looked for the other door.

We would not enjoy the wonderful series *Fairytale Theater* if actress-producer Shelley Duvall had stayed home complaining during acting droughts instead of turning her creativity elsewhere. *Non illegitimi te carborundum*, the graffiti in prisoner-of-war camps is said to have run. The rough translation, very important for artists, is "Don't let the bastards get you down."

Artists who take this to heart survive and often prevail. The key here is action. Pain that is not used profitably quickly solidifies into a leaden heart, which makes *any* action difficult.

When faced with a loss, immediately take one small action to support your artist. Even if all you are doing is buying a bunch of tulips and a sketch pad, your action says, "I acknowledge you and your pain. I promise you a future worth having." Like a small child, our artist needs mommying. "Ouch. That hurt. Here's a little treat, a lullaby, a promise . . ."

I have a director friend who tells me that on his worst nights, when he is about to open a new film and he awaits career catastrophe, sure that he will never work again, in the dark, alone, he cajoles himself to sleep: "If I can't shoot 35 mm, I could still shoot 16 mm. If I can't shoot 16 mm, then I can shoot video. If I can't shoot video, I can shoot super 8."

AGE AND TIME: PRODUCT AND PROCESS

QUESTION: Do you know how old I'll be by the time I learn
to play the piano?

ANSWER: The same age you will be if you don't.

"I'm too old for that" ranks with "I don't have money for
it" as a Great Block Lie we use to prevent further exploration.
"I'm too old" is something we tell ourselves to save ourselves
from the emotional cost of the ego deflation involved in being
a beginner.

"I'm too old to go to film school," I told myself at thirty-
five. And when I got to film school I discovered that I was indeed fifteen years older than my classmates. I also discovered I
had greater creative hunger, more life experience, and a much
stronger learning curve. Now that I've taught in a film school
myself, I find that very often my best students are those who
came to their work late.

"I'm too old to be an actor," I have heard many students
complain—and dramatically, I might add. They are not always
pleased when I tell them this is not the case. The splendid actor
John Mahoney did not begin acting until he was nearly forty.
Ten years into a highly successful career, he is now often
booked three films in advance and works with some of the
finest directors in the world.

"I'm too old to really be a writer" is another frequent complaint. This is more ego-saving nonsense. Raymond Chandler
didn't publish until the far side of forty. The superb novel *Jules
and Jim* was written as a first novel by a man in his seventies.

, "I'm too old" is an evasive tactic. It is *always* used to avoid
facing fear.

Now let's look at the other side: "I'll let myself try it when
I'm retired." This is an interesting side trip on the same ego-
saving track. As a culture, we glorify youth and allow our
youth the freedom to experiment. And we disparage our old-
timers but allow them the right to be a little crazy.

Many blocked creatives tell themselves they are both too
old and too young to allow themselves to pursue their dreams.
Old and dotty, they might try it. Young and foolish, they
might try it. In either scenario, being crazy is a prerequisite to

creative exploration. We do not want to look crazy. And trying something like that (whatever it is) at our age (whatever it is) would look nuts.

Yes, maybe.

Creativity occurs in the moment, and in the moment we are timeless. We discover that as we engage in a creative recovery. "I felt like a kid," we may say after a satisfying artist date. Kids are not self-conscious, and once we are actually in the flow of our creativity, neither are we.

"How long would it take me to learn to do that?" we may ask, standing on the sideline of a longed-for activity.

"Maybe a year to be pretty good," the answer comes back. "It depends."

As blocked creatives, we like to pretend that a year or even several years is a long, long time. Our ego plays this little trick to keep us from getting started. Instead of allowing ourselves a creative journey, we focus on the length of the trip. "It's such a long way," we tell ourselves. It may be, but each day is just one more day with some motion in it, and that motion toward a goal is very enjoyable.

At the heart of the anorexia of artistic avoidance is the denial of process. We like to focus on having learned a skill or on having made an artwork. This attention to final form ignores the fact that creativity lies not in the done but in doing.

"I am writing a screenplay" is infinitely more interesting to the soul than "I have written a screenplay," which pleases the ego. "I am in an acting class" is infinitely more interesting than "I took an acting class a few years ago."

In a sense, no creative act is ever finished. You can't learn to act because there is always more to learn. Arguably, you cannot even direct a film because you will always be redirecting it, even years later. You will know then what you might have done and what you will do next if you keep working. This doesn't mean that the work accomplished is worthless. Far from it. It simply means that doing the work points the way to new and better work to be done.

Focused on process, our creative life retains a sense of adventure. Focused on product, the same creative life can feel foolish or barren. We inherit the obsession with product and the idea that art produces finished product from our consumer-oriented society. This focus creates a great deal of creative block. We, as working artists, may want to explore a new artistic area, but we don't see where it will get us. We wonder if it will be good for our career. Fixated on the need to have something to show for our labors, we often deny our curiosities. Every time we do this, we are blocked.

Our use of age as a block to creative work interlocks with our toxic finished-product thinking. We have set an appropriate age on certain activities: college graduation, going to med school, writing a first book. This artificial ego requirement asks us to be done when what we truly yearn for is to start something.

"If I didn't think I'd look like a jerk next to the young guys, I'd let myself sign up for an improv class."

"If my body looked anything the way it did twenty years ago, I'd let myself take that jazzercize class at the Y."

"If I didn't think my family would consider me a stupid old fool, I'd start playing the piano again. I still remember some of my lessons."

If these excuses are beginning to sound flimsy to you, good! Ask yourself if you haven't employed a few of them. Then ask yourself if you can acquire the humility to start something despite your ego's reservations.

The grace to be a beginner is always the best prayer for an artist. The beginner's humility and openness lead to exploration. Exploration leads to accomplishment. All of it begins at the beginning, with the first small and scary step.

FILLING THE FORM

What do I mean by *filling the form*? I mean taking the next small step instead of skipping ahead to a large one for which you may not yet be prepared. To be very specific, in order to sell a screenplay, you must first write one. In order to write one, you must come up with an idea and then commit it to paper, a page at a time until you have about 120 pages of script. *Filling the form* means that you write your daily pages. It means that when

There is a logic of colors, and it is with this alone, and not with the logic of the brain, that the painter should conform.

PAUL CÉZANNE

obsession strikes—as it will—about how the damn thing is not any good, you tell yourself that this is a question for later and turn back to doing what is the next right thing. And that means you write the pages of the day.

If you break a screenplay down into daily increments, that small smattering of writing can get done quickly and promptly—before the dirty laundry. And it can carry you through the rest of your day guilt-free and less anxious.

Art? You just do it.

MARTIN RITT

Most of the time, the next right thing is something small: washing out your paintbrushes, stopping by the art-supply store and getting your clay, checking the local paper for a list of acting classes . . . As a rule of thumb, it is best to just admit that there is always *one* action you can take for your creativity daily. This daily-action commitment fills the form.

All too often, when people look to having a more creative life, they hold an unspoken and often unacknowledged expectation, or fear, that they will be abandoning life as they know it.

"I can't be a writer and stay in this marriage."

"I can't pursue my painting and stay at this dull job."

"I can't commit to acting and stay in Chicago . . . or Seattle or Atlanta . . ."

Blocked creatives like to think they are looking at changing their whole life in one fell swoop. This form of grandiosity is very often its own undoing. By setting the jumps too high and making the price tag too great, the recovering artist sets defeat in motion. Who can concentrate on a first drawing class when he is obsessing about having to divorce his wife and leave town? Who can turn toe out in modern jazz form when she is busy reading the ads for a new apartment since she will have to break up with her lover to concentrate on her art?

Creative people are dramatic, and we use negative drama to scare ourselves out of our creativity with this notion of wholesale and often destructive change. Fantasizing about pursuing our art full-time, we fail to pursue it part-time—or at all.

Instead of writing three pages a day on a screenplay, we prefer worrying about how we will have to move to Hollywood if the script gets bought. Which it can't anyway since we are too busy worrying about selling it to write it.

Instead of checking into a life-drawing class at the local

culture center, we buy *Art Forum* and remind ourselves that our stuff is not in style. How can it be? It doesn't exist yet!

Instead of clearing out the little room off the kitchen so that we will have a place to work on our pottery, we complain about needing a studio—a complaint that we ourselves cannot take seriously since we do not have any work to argue our case.

Indulging ourselves in a frantic fantasy of what our life would look like if we were *real* artists, we fail to see the many small creative changes that we could make at this very moment. This kind of look-at-the-big-picture thinking ignores the fact that a creative life is grounded on many, many small steps and very, very few large leaps.

Rather than take a scary baby step toward our dreams, we rush to the edge of the cliff and then stand there, quaking, saying, "I can't leap. I can't. I can't. . . ."

No one is asking you to leap. That's just drama, and, for the purposes of a creative recovery, drama belongs on the page or on the canvas or in the clay or in the acting class or in the *act* of creativity, however small.

Creativity requires activity, and this is not good news to most of us. It makes us responsible, and we tend to hate that. You mean I have to *do* something in order to feel better?

Yes. And most of us hate to *do* something when we can obsess about something else instead. One of our favorite things to do—instead of our art—is to contemplate the odds.

In a creative career, thinking about the odds is a drink of emotional poison. It robs us of the dignity of art-as-process and puts us at the mercy of imagined powers *out there*. Taking this drink quickly leads to a severe and toxic emotional bender. It leads us to ask, "What's the use?" instead of "What next?"

As a rule of thumb, the odds are what we use to procrastinate about doing what comes next. This is our addiction to anxiety in lieu of action. Once you catch on to this, the jig is up. Watch yourself for a week and notice the way you will pick up an anxious thought, almost like a joint, to blow off—or at least delay—your next creative action.

You've cleared a morning to write or paint but then you realize that the clothes are dirty. "I'll just think about what I want to paint and fine-tune it while I fold the clothes," you tell yourself. What you really mean is, "Instead of painting any-thing, I will worry about it some more." Somehow, the laun-dry takes your whole morning.

Most blocked creatives have an active addiction to anxiety. We prefer the low-grade pain and occasional heart-stopping panic attack to the drudgery of small and simple daily steps in the right direction.

Filling the form means that we must work with what we have rather than languish in complaints over what we have not. As a director, I have noticed that the actors who get work are the actors who *work*—whether they are working or not. I am thinking specifically about Marge Kottlisky, a fine stage and film actress who has always made herself available to work and to workshop writers' materials. She worked with the young playwright David Mamet in the St. Nicholas Theater Group in Chicago and now works with the somewhat older and more accomplished David Mamet wherever he is working. Rather than rest on any creative laurels, she engages in a very healthy sort of creative restlessness. When she is not engaged in the run of a show, she often takes a class to keep her hand in, and she always is available for read-throughs of new plays. Like all actors, she suffers from the "I'll never work again" syndrome, but unlike many less-committed actors, she never allows her-self to make her work something she does only for others or only when she is paid. Yes, she wants to be paid, and I am not arguing here that actors should work for free. What I am say-ing is that work begets work. Small actions lead us to the larger movements in our creative lives.

Many actors allow themselves the dubious luxury of hand-ing their careers over to their agents instead of keeping their art in the custody of their souls. When an agent is in charge of your creative life, you can easily despair that "my agent doesn't do enough" instead of asking what you yourself might do to hone your craft. Fill the form. What can you do, right now, in your life as it is currently constituted? Do that thing.

Take one small daily action instead of indulging in the big questions. When we allow ourselves to wallow in the big ques-tions, we fail to find the small answers. What we are talking about here is a concept of change grounded in respect—respect

for where we are as well as where we wish to go. We are looking not to grand strokes of change—although they may
come—but instead to the act of creatively husbanding all that
is in the present: this job, this house, this relationship.

Recovering creatives commonly undergo bouts of fierce
rage and grief over their lost years. When these creative kriyas
occur, we desperately want to kick over the traces and get the
hell out of life as it is currently constituted. Instead, make
changes, small changes, right where you are. Fill this form
with creative care until it overflows into a newer, larger form—
organically.

As the poet Theodore Roethke phrases it, "We learn by
going/Where we have to go." We have found that when we fill
the form, we do not often need to make large changes. Large
changes occur in tiny increments. It is useful to think in terms
of a space flight: by altering the launch trajectory very slightly,
a great difference can be made over time.

EARLY PATTERNINGS, AN EXERCISE

Although we seldom connect the dots, many of our present-
day losses are connected to our earlier conditioning. Children
may be told they can't do anything or, equally damaging, be
told they should be able to do absolutely anything with ease.
Either of these messages blocks the recipient. The following
questions are aimed at helping you retrieve and decipher your
own conditioning. Some of them may seem not to apply. Write
about *whatever* they trigger for you.

1. As a kid, my dad thought my art was _____. That
   made me feel _____.

2. I remember one time when he _____.

3. I felt very _____ and _____ about that. I never forgot it.

4. As a kid, my mother taught me that my daydreaming
   was _____.

5. I remember she'd tell me to snap out of it by reminding me _____.

6. The person I remember who believed in me was ____.

7. I remember one time when _____.

8. I felt _____ and _____ about that. I never forgot it.

I am in the world only for the purpose of composing.

FRANZ SCHUBERT

9. The thing that ruined my chance to be an artist was _____

10. The negative lesson I got from that, which wasn't logical but I still believe, is that I can't _____ and be an artist.

11. When I was little, I learned that _____ and _____ were big sins that I particularly had to watch out for.

12. I grew up thinking artists were _____ people.

13. The teacher who shipwrecked my confidence was _____.

14. I was told _____.

15. I believed this teacher because _____.

16. The mentor who gave me a good role model was ____.

17. When people say I have talent I think they want to _____.

18. The thing is, I am suspicious that _____.

19. I just can't believe that _____.

20. If I believe I am really talented, then I am mad as hell at _____ and _____ and _____ and _____ and _____.

AFFIRMATIONS

The following affirmations affirm your right to the practice of your creativity. Select five affirmations and work with them this week.

I am a talented person.
I have a right to be an artist.
I am a good person and a good artist.
Creativity is a blessing I accept.
My creativity blesses others.
My creativity is appreciated.
I now treat myself and my creativity more gently.
I now treat myself and my creativity more generously.
I now share my creativity more openly.
I now accept hope.
I now act affirmatively.
I now accept creative recovery.
I now allow myself to heal.
I now accept God's help unfolding my life.
I now believe God loves artists.

TASKS ✉

1. Goal Search: You may find the following exercise difficult. Allow yourself to do it anyway. If multiple dreams occur to you, do the exercise for each one of them. The simple act of imagining a dream in concrete detail helps us to bring it into reality. Think of your goal search as a preliminary architect's drawing for the life you would wish to have.

The Steps

1. Name your dream. That's right. Write it down. "In a perfect world, I would secretly love to be a _____."
2. Name one concrete goal that signals to you its accomplishment. On your emotional compass, this goal signifies true north.

   (Note: two people may want to be an actress. They

share that dream. For one, an article in *People* magazine is the concrete goal. To her, glamour is the emotional center for her dream; glamour is true north. For the second actress, the concrete goal is a good review in a Broadway play. To her, respect as a creative artist is the emotional center of her dream; respect is true north. Actress one might be happy as a soap star. Actress two would need stage work to fulfill her dream. On the surface, both seem to desire the same thing.)

3. In a perfect world, where would you like to be in five years in relation to your dream and true north?

4. In the world we inhabit now, what action can you take, this year, to move you closer?

5. What action can you take this month? This week? This day? Right now?

6. List your dream (for example, to be a famous film director). List its true north (respect and higher consciousness, mass communication.) Select a role model (Walt Disney, Ron Howard, Michael Powell). Make an action plan. Five years. Three years. One year. One month. One week. Now. Choose an action. *Reading this book is an action.*

2. New Childhood: What might you have been if you'd had perfect nurturing? Write a page of this fantasy childhood. What were you given? Can you reparent yourself in that direction now?

3. Color Schemes: Pick a color and write a quick few sentences describing yourself in the first person. ("I am silver, high-tech and ethereal, the color of dreams and accomplishment, the color of half-light and in between, I feel serene." Or "I am red. I am passion, sunset, anger, blood, wine and roses, armies, murder, lust, and apples." What is your favorite color? What do you have that is that color? What about an entire room? This is your life and your house.

> *Your desire is your prayer. Picture the fulfillment of your desire now and feel its reality and you will experience the joy of the answered prayer.*
>
> DR. JOSEPH MURPHY

4. List five things you are not allowed to do: kill your boss, scream in church, go outside naked, make a scene, quit your job. Now do that thing on paper. Write it, draw it, paint it, act it out, collage it. Now put some music on and dance it.

5. Style Search: List twenty things you like to do. (Perhaps the same twenty you listed before, perhaps not.) Answer these questions for each item.
   Does it cost money or is it free?
   Expensive or cheap?
   Alone or with somebody?
   Job related?
   Physical risk?
   Fast-paced or slow?
   Mind, body, or spiritual?

6. Ideal Day: Plan a perfect day in your life as it is now constituted, using the information gleaned from above.

7. Ideal Ideal Day: Plan a perfect day in your life as you *wish* it were constituted. There are no restrictions. Allow yourself to be and to have whatever your heart desires. Your ideal environment, job, home, circle of friends, intimate relationship, stature in your art form— your wildest dreams.

8. Choose one festive aspect from your ideal day. Allow yourself to live it. You may not be able to move to Rome yet, but even in a still-grungy apartment you can enjoy a homemade cappuccino and a croissant.

CHECK-IN ✐

1. How many days this week did you do your morning pages? (Have you been very tempted to abandon them?) How was the experience for you?

2. Did you do your artist date this week? (Have you been allowing workaholism or other commitments to sabotage this practice?) What did you do? How did it feel?

3. Did you experience any synchronicity this week? What was it?

4. Were there any other issues this week that you consider significant for your recovery? Describe them.

Recovering a Sense of Compassion

This week finds us facing the internal blocks to creativity. It may be tempting to abandon ship at this point. Don't! We will explore and acknowledge the emotional difficulties that beset us in the past as we made creative efforts. We will undertake healing the shame of past failures. We will gain in compassion as we reparent the frightened artist child who yearns for creative accomplishment. We will learn tools to dismantle emotional blocks and support renewed risk.

FEAR

ONE OF THE MOST important tasks in artistic recovery is learning to call things—and ourselves—by the right names. Most of us have spent years using the wrong names for our behaviors. We have wanted to create and we have been unable to create and we have called that inability *laziness.* This is not merely inaccurate. It is cruel. Accuracy and compassion serve us far better.

Blocked artists are not lazy. They are blocked.

Being blocked and being lazy are two different things. The blocked artist typically expends a great deal of energy—just not visibly. The blocked artist spends energy on self-hatred, on regret, on grief, and on jealousy. The blocked artist spends energy on self-doubt.

The blocked artist does not know how to begin with baby steps. Instead, the blocked artist thinks in terms of great big scary impossible tasks: a novel, a feature film, a one-person show, an opera. When these large tasks are not accomplished, or even begun, the blocked artist calls that laziness.

Do not call the inability to start laziness. Call it fear.

Fear is the true name for what ails the blocked artist. It may be fear of failure or fear of success. Most frequently, it is fear of abandonment. This fear has roots in childhood reality. Most blocked artists tried to become artists against either their parents' good wishes or their parents' good judgment. For a youngster this is quite a conflict. To go squarely against your parents' values means you'd better know what you're doing. You'd better not just be an artist. You better be a *great* artist if you're going to hurt your parents so much. . . .

Parents do act hurt when children rebel, and declaring oneself an artist is usually viewed by parents as an act of rebellion. Unfortunately, the view of an artist's life as an adolescent rebellion often lingers, making any act of art entail the risk of separation and the loss of loved ones. Because artists still yearn for their creative goals, they then feel guilty.

This guilt demands that they set a goal for themselves right off the bat that they must be great artists in order to justify this rebellion.

The need to be a great artist makes it hard to be an artist.

The need to produce a great work of art makes it hard to produce any art at all.

Finding it hard to begin a project does not mean you will not be able to do it. It means you will need help—from your higher power, from supportive friends, and from yourself. First of all, you must give yourself permission to begin small and go in baby steps. These steps must be rewarded. Setting impossible goals creates enormous fear, which creates procrastination, which we wrongly call laziness.

Do not call procrastination laziness. Call it fear.

Fear is what blocks an artist. The fear of not being good enough. The fear of not finishing. The fear of failure and of success. The fear of beginning at all. There is only one cure for fear. That cure is love.

Use love for your artist to cure its fear.

Stop yelling at yourself. Be nice. Call fear by its right name.

ENTHUSIASM

"It must take so much discipline to be an artist," we are often told by well-meaning people who are not artists but wish they were. What a temptation. What a seduction. They're inviting us to preen before an admiring audience, to act out the image that is so heroic and Spartan—and false.

It don't mean a thing if it ain't got that swing.

DUKE ELLINGTON
AND IRVING MILLS

As artists, grounding our self-image in military discipline is dangerous. In the short run, discipline may work, but it will work only for a while. By its very nature, discipline is rooted in self-admiration. (Think of discipline as a battery, useful but short-lived.) We admire ourselves for being so wonderful. The discipline itself, not the creative outflow, becomes the point.

That part of us that creates best is not a driven, disciplined automaton, functioning from willpower, with a booster of pride to back it up. This is operating out of self-will. You know the image: rising at dawn with military precision, saluting the desk, the easel, the drawing board . . .

Over any extended period of time, being an artist requires enthusiasm more than discipline. Enthusiasm is not an emotional state. It is a spiritual commitment, a loving surrender to our creative process, a loving recognition of all the creativity around us.

Enthusiasm (from the Greek, "filled with God") is an ongoing energy supply tapped into the flow of life itself. Enthusiasm is grounded in play, not work. Far from being a brain-numbed soldier, our artist is actually our child within, our inner playmate. As with all playmates, it is joy, not duty, that makes for a lasting bond.

True, our artist may rise at dawn to greet the typewriter or easel in the morning stillness. But this event has more to do with a child's love of secret adventure than with ironclad discipline. What other people may view as discipline is actually a play date that we make with our artist child: "I'll meet you at 6:00 A.M. and we'll goof around with that script, painting, sculpture . . ."

Our artist child can best be enticed to work by treating work as play. Paint is great gooey stuff. Sixty sharpened pencils are fun. Many writers eschew a computer for the comforting, companionable clatter for a solid typewriter that trots along like a pony. In order to work well, many artists find that their work spaces are best dealt with as play spaces.

Dinosaur murals, toys from the five-and-dime, tiny miniature Christmas lights, papier-mâché monsters, hanging crystals, a sprig of flowers, a fish tank . . .

As attractive as the idea of a pristine cell, monastic in its severity, is to our romanticized notion of being a real artist, the workable truth may be somewhat messier than that. Most little kids would be bored silly in a stark, barren room. Our artist child is no exception.

Remember that art is process. The process is supposed to be fun. For our purposes, "the journey is always the only arrival" may be interpreted to mean that our creative work is actually our creativity itself at play in the field of time. At the heart of this play is the mystery of joy.

CREATIVE U-TURNS

Recovering from artist's block, like recovering from any major illness or injury, requires a commitment to health. At some point, we must make an active choice to relinquish the joys and privileges accorded to the emotional invalid. A productive artist is quite often a happy person. This can be very threatening as a self-concept to those who are used to getting their needs met by being unhappy.

"I'd love to, but you see . . . I have these crippling fears . . ." can get us a lot of attention. We get more sympathy as crippled artists than as functional ones. Those of us addicted to sympathy in the place of creativity can become increasingly threatened as we become increasingly functional. Many recovering artists become so threatened that they make U-turns and sabotage themselves.

We usually commit creative hara-kiri either on the eve of or in the wake of a first creative victory. The glare of success (a poem, an acting job, a song, a short story, a film, or any success) can send the recovering artist scurrying back into the cave of self-defeat. We're more comfortable being a victim of artist's

Art evokes the mystery without which the world would not exist.

RENÉ-FRANÇOIS-GHISLAIN MAGRITTE

block than risking having to consistently be productive and healthy.

An artistic U-turn arrives on a sudden wave of indifference. We greet our newly minted product or our delightful process with "Aw, what does it matter anyhow? It's just a start. Everybody else is so much further ahead. . . ."

Yes, and they will stay that way if we stop working. The point is we have traveled light-years from where we were when we were blocked. We are now on the road, and the road is scary. We begin to be distracted by roadside attractions or detoured by the bumps.

Man is not free to refuse to do the thing which gives him more pleasure than any other conceivable action.

STENDHAL

- A screenwriter has an agent interested in repping a script with just a few changes. He doesn't make the changes.

- A performance artist is offered a space to use for workshopping his new material. He does it once, doesn't like his mixed reception indicating more work is needed, then stops working on new material at all.

- An actor is told to get his head shots together and check back in with a prestigious agent. He doesn't get his head shots, doesn't check back in.

- An actress-producer with a solid script is offered a studio deal to further develop her project. She finds fault with the deal and then shelves the project entirely.

- A painter is invited into a group show, his first, but picks a fight with the gallery owner.

- A poet reads some poems to very good public reception at a neighborhood open mike. Instead of continuing at this level and gaining strength, the poet enters a *slam* (a sort of boxing match for poets judged by nonpoets), loses, and stops reading publicly altogether.

- A lyricist hooks up with a new composer, and they literally make beautiful music together. They demo three songs, which get enthusiastic response, and then stop working together.

• A fledgling photographer is greatly encouraged by her teacher's interest in her work. She botches developing one roll of film and then quits the class, claiming it was boring.

Life shrinks or expands in proportion to one's courage.

ANAÏS NIN

In dealing with our creative U-turns, we must first of all extend ourselves some sympathy. Creativity is scary, and in *all* careers there are U-turns. Sometimes these U-turns are best viewed as recycling times. We come up to a creative jump, run out from it like a skittish horse, then circle the field a few times before trying the fence again.

Typically, when we take a creative U-turn we are doubly shamed: first by our fear and second by our reaction to it. Again, let me say it helps to remember that *all* careers have them.

For two years in my mid-thirties I wrote arts coverage for the *Chicago Tribune*. In this capacity, I talked to Akira Kurosawa, Kevin Klein, Julie Andrews, Jane Fonda, Blake Edwards, Sydney Pollack, Sissy Spacek, Sigourney Weaver, Martin Ritt, Gregory Hines, and fifty-odd more. I talked to most of them about discouragement—which meant talking to them about U-turns. As much as talent, the capacity to avoid or recoup from creative U-turns distinguished their careers.

A successful creative career is always built on successful creative failures. The trick is to survive them. It helps to remember that even our most illustrious artists have taken creative U-turns in their time.

Blake Edwards has directed some of the funniest and most successful comedy of the past three decades. Nonetheless, he spent seven years in self-imposed exile in Switzerland because a script that he felt was his best was taken away from him in preproduction when his take on the material differed from that of the star the studio had acquired to enhance it.

Fired from his own project, Edwards sat on the sidelines watching as his beloved film was made by others and botched badly. Like a wounded panther, Edwards retired to the Alps to nurse his wounds. He wound up back directing seven long years later—when he concluded that creativity, not time, would best heal his creative wounds. Sticking to this philosophy, he has been aggressively productive every since. Talking about this time-out to me, he was rueful, and pained, about the time it cost him.

Have compassion. Creative U-turns are always born from fear—fear of success or fear of failure. It doesn't really matter which. The net result is the same.

To recover from a creative U-turn, or a pattern involving many creative U-turns, we must first admit that it exists. Yes, I did react negatively to fear and pain. Yes, I do need help.

Think of your talent as a young and skittish horse that you are bringing along. This horse is very talented but it is also young, nervous, and inexperienced. It will make mistakes, be frightened by obstacles it hasn't seen before. It may even bolt, try to throw you off, feign lameness. Your job, as the creative jockey, is to keep your horse moving forward and to coax it into finishing the course.

First of all, take a look at what jumps make your horse so skittish. You may find that certain obstacles are far more scary than others. An agent jump may frighten you more than a workshop jump. A review jump may be okay while a rewrite jump scares your talent to death. Remember that in a horse race, there are other horses in the field. One trick a seasoned jockey uses is to place a green horse in the slipstream of an older, steadier, and more seasoned horse. You can do this, too.

- Who do I know who has an agent? Then ask them how they got one.

- Who do I know who has done a successful rewrite? Ask them how to do one.

- Do I know anyone who has survived a savage review? Ask them what they did to heal themselves.

Once we admit the need for help, the help arrives. The ego always wants to claim self-sufficiency. It would rather pose as a creative loner than ask for help. Ask anyway.

Bob was a promising young director when he made his first documentary. It was a short, very powerful film about his father, a factory worker. When he had a rough cut together,

Bob showed it to a teacher, a once-gifted filmmaker who was blocked himself. The teacher savaged it. Bob abandoned the film. He stuck the film in some boxes, stuck the boxes in his basement, and forgot about them until the basement flooded. "Oh well. Just as well," he told himself then, assuming the film was ruined.

I met Bob half a decade later. Sometime after we became friends, he told me the story of his film. I had a suspicion that it was good. "It's lost," he told me. "Even the lab lost the footage I gave them." Talking about the film, Bob broke down—and through. He began to mourn his abandoned dream.

A week later, Bob got a call from the lab. "It's incredible. They found the footage," he related. I was not too surprised. I believe the creator keeps an eye on artists and was protecting that film. With the encouragement of his screenwriter girl-friend, now his wife, Bob finished his film. They have gone on to make a second, innovative documentary together.

Faced with a creative U-turn, ask yourself, "Who can I ask for help about this U-turn?" Then start asking.

BLASTING THROUGH BLOCKS

In order to work freely on a project, an artist must be at least functionally free of resentment (anger) and resistance (fear). What do we mean by that? We mean that any buried barriers must be aired before the work can proceed. The same holds true for any buried payoffs to not working. Blocks are seldom mysterious. They are, instead, recognizable artistic defenses against what is perceived (rightly or wrongly) as a hostile environment.

Remember, your artist is a creative child. It sulks, throws tantrums, holds grudges, harbors irrational fears. Like most children, it is afraid of the dark, the bogeyman, and any adventure that isn't safely scary. As your artist's parent and guardian, its big brother, warrior, and companion, it falls to you to convince your artist it is safe to come out and (work) play.

Beginning any new project, it's a good idea to ask your artist a few simple questions. These questions will help remove common bugaboos standing between your artist and the work. These same questions, asked when work grows difficult or bogs down, usually act to clear the obstructed flow.

1. List any resentments (anger) you have in connection with this project. It does not matter how petty, picky, or irrational these resentments may appear to your adult self. To your artist child they are real big deals: grudges.

   Some examples: I resent being the second artist asked, not the first. (I am too the best.) . . . I resent this editor, she just nitpicks. She never says anything nice. . . . I resent doing work for this idiot; he never pays me on time.

2. Ask your artist to list any and all fears about the projected piece of work and/or anyone connected to it. Again, these fears can be as dumb as any two-year-old's. It does not matter that they are groundless to your adult's eye. What matters it that they are big scary monsters to your artist.

   Some examples: I'm afraid the work will be rotten and I won't know it. . . . I'm afraid the work will be good and they won't know it. . . . I'm afraid all my ideas are hackneyed and outdated. . . . I'm afraid my ideas are ahead of their time. . . . I'm afraid I'll starve. . . . I'm afraid I'll never finish. . . . I'm afraid I'll never start. . . . I'm afraid I will be embarrassed (I'm already embarrassed). . . . The list goes on.

3. Ask yourself if that is all. Have you left out any itsy fear? Have you suppressed any "stupid" anger? Get it on the page.

4. Ask yourself what you stand to gain by not doing this piece of work.

   Some examples: If I don't write the piece, no one can hate it. . . . If I don't write the piece, my jerk editor will worry. . . . If I don't paint, sculpt, act, sing, dance, I can criticize others, knowing I could do better.

Music is your own experience, your thoughts, your wisdom. If you don't live it, it won't come out your horn.

CHARLIE PARKER

5. Make your deal. The deal is: "Okay, Creative Force, you take care of the quality, I'll take care of the quantity." Sign your deal and post it.

A word of warning: this is a very powerful exercise; it can do fatal damage to a creative block.

Be really whole
And all things will come to you.

LAO-TZU

TASKS ✉

1. Read your morning pages! This process is best undertaken with two colored markers, one to highlight insights and another to highlight actions needed. Do not judge your pages or yourself. This is very important. Yes, they will be boring. Yes, they may be painful. Consider them a map. Take them as information, not an indictment.

   Take Stock: Who have you consistently been complaining about? What have you procrastinated on? What blessedly have you allowed yourself to change or accept?

   Take Heart: Many of us notice an alarming tendency toward black-and-white thinking: "He's terrible. He's wonderful. I love him. I hate him. It's a great job. It's a terrible job," and so forth. Don't be thrown by this.

   Acknowledge: The pages have allowed us to vent without self-destruction, to plan without interference, to complain without an audience, to dream without restriction, to know our own minds. Give yourself credit for undertaking them. Give them credit for the changes and growth they have fostered.

2. Visualizing: You have already done work with naming your goal and identifying true north. The following exercise asks you to fully imagine having your goal accomplished. Please spend enough time to fill in the juicy details that would really make the experience wonderful for you.

Name your goal: I am _____.

In the present tense, describe yourself doing it at the height of your powers! This is your ideal scene.

Read this aloud to yourself.

Post this above your work area.

Read this aloud, daily!

For the next week collect actual pictures of yourself and combine them with magazine images to collage your ideal scene described above. Remember, seeing is believing, and the added visual cue of your real self in your ideal scene can make it far more real.

3. Priorities: List for yourself your creative goals for the year. List for yourself your creative goals for the month. List for yourself your creative goals for the week.

4. Creative U-Turns: All of us have taken creative U-turns. Name one of yours. Name three more. Name the one that just kills you.

   Forgive yourself. Forgive yourself for all failures of nerve, timing, and initiative. Devise a personalized list of affirmations to help you do better in the future.

   Very gently, *very gently,* consider whether any aborted, abandoned, savaged, or sabotaged brainchildren can be rescued. Remember, you are not alone. All of us have taken creative U-turns.

   Choose one creative U-turn. Retrieve it. Mend it.

   Do not take a creative U-turn now. Instead, notice your resistance. Morning pages seeming difficult? Stupid? Pointless? Too obvious? Do them anyway.

   What creative dreams are lurching toward possibility? Admit that they frighten you.

   Choose an artist totem. It might be a doll, a stuffed animal, a carved figuring, or a wind-up toy. The point is to choose something you immediately feel a protective fondness toward. Give your totem a place of honor and then honor it by not beating up on your artist child.

Learning is movement from moment to moment.

    J. KRISHNAMURTI

*We learn to do something by
doing it. There is no other way.*

JOHN HOLT
EDUCATOR

CHECK-IN 🖉

1. How many days this week you do your morning pages? Regarding your U-turns, have you allowed yourself a shift toward compassion, at least on the page?

2. Did you do your artist date this week? Have you kept the emphasis on fun? What did you do? How did it feel?

3. Did you experience any synchronicity this week? What was it?

4. Were there any other issues this week that you consider significant for your recovery? Describe them.

Recovering a Sense of Self-Protection

This week we explore the perils that can ambush us on our creative path. Because creativity is a spiritual issue, many of the perils are spiritual perils. In the essays, tasks, and exercises of this week, we search out the toxic patterns we cling to that block our creative flow.

DANGERS OF THE TRAIL

CREATIVITY IS GOD ENERGY flowing through us, shaped by us, like light flowing through a crystal prism. When we are clear about who we are and what we are doing, the energy flows freely and we experience no strain. When we resist what that energy might show us or where it might take us, we often experience a shaky, out-of-control feeling. We want to shut down the flow and regain our sense of control. We slam on the psychic brakes.

Every creative person has myriad ways to block creativity. Each of us favors one or two ways particularly toxic to us because they block us so effectively.

For some people, food is a creativity issue. Eating sugar or fats or certain carbohydrates may leave them feeling dulled, hung over, unable to focus—blurry. They use food to block energy and change. As the shaky feeling comes over them that they are going too fast and God knows where, that they are about to fly apart, these people reach for food. A big bowl of ice cream, an evening of junk food, and their system clogs: What was I thinking? What . . . ? Oh, never mind. . . .

For some people alcohol is the favored block. For others, drugs. For many, work is the block of choice. Busy, busy, busy, they grab for tasks to numb themselves with. They can't take a half hour's walk. "What a waste of time!" Must-dos and multiple projects are drawn to them like flies to a soda can in the sun. They go, "Buzz, buzz, buzz, *swat!*" as they brush aside the stray thought that was the breakthrough insight.

For others, an obsession with painful love places creative choice outside their hands. Reaching for the painful thought, they become instant victims rather than feel their own considerable power. "If only he or she would just love me . . ."

This obsessive thought drowns out the little voice that suggests rearranging the living room, taking a pottery class, trying a new top on that story that's stymied. The minute a creative thought raises its head, it is lopped off by the obsession, which blocks fear and prevents risk. Going out dancing? Redoing the whole play with an inner-city theme? "If only he or she would love me . . ." So much for *West Side Story.*

Sex is the great block for many. A mesmerizing, titillating hypnotic interest slides novel erotic possibilities in front of the real novel. The new sex object becomes the focus for creative approaches.

Now, note carefully that food, work, and sex are all good in themselves. It is the *abuse* of them that makes them creativity issues. Knowing yourself as an artist means acknowledging which of these you abuse when you want to block yourself. If creativity is like a burst of the universe's breath through the straw that is each of us, we pinch that straw whenever we pick up one of our blocks. We shut down our flow. And we do it on purpose.

We begin to sense our real potential and the wide range of possibilities open to us. That scares us. So we all reach for blocks to slow our growth. If we are honest with ourselves, we all know which blocks are the toxic ones for us. Clue: this is the block we defend as our right.

Saying no can be the ultimate self-care.

CLAUDIA BLACK

Line up the possibilities. Which one makes you angry to even think about giving up? That explosive one is the one that has caused you the most derailment. Examine it. When asked to name our poison, most of us can. Has food sabotaged me? Has workaholism sabotaged me? Has sex or love obsession blocked my creativity?

Mix and match is a common recipe for using blocks: use one, add another, mix in a third, wear yourself out. The object of all of this blocking is to alleviate fear. We turn to our drug of choice to block our creativity whenever we experience the anxiety of our inner emptiness. It is always fear—often disguised but *always* there—that leads us into grabbing for a block.

Usually, we experience the choice to block as a coincidence. She happened to call . . . I felt hungry and there was some ice cream . . . He dropped by with some killer dope. . . . The choice to block always works in the short run and fails in the long run.

The choice to block is a creative U-turn. We turn back on ourselves. Like water forced to a standstill, we turn stagnant. The self-honesty lurking in us all always knows when we choose against our greater good. It marks a little jot on our spiritual blackboard: "Did it again."

It takes grace and courage to admit and surrender our blocking devices. Who wants to? Not while they are still working! Of course, long after they have stopped working, we hope against hope that this time they will work again.

Blocking is essentially an issue of faith. Rather than trust our intuition, our talent, our skill, our desire, we fear where our creator is taking us with this creativity. Rather than paint, write, dance, audition, and see where it takes us, we pick up a block. Blocked, we know who and what we are: unhappy people. Unblocked, we may be something much more threatening—happy. For most of us, happy is terrifying, unfamiliar, out of control, too risky! Is it any wonder we take temporary U-turns?

As we become aware of our blocking devices—food, busyness, alcohol, sex, other drugs—we can feel our U-turns as we make them. The blocks will no longer work effectively. Over time, we will try—perhaps slowly at first and erratically—to

In the middle of difficulty lies opportunity.

ALBERT EINSTEIN

ride out the anxiety and see where we emerge. Anxiety is fuel. We can use it to write with, paint with, work with.

> *Feel: anxious!*
> *Try: using the anxiety!*
> *Feel: I just did it! I didn't block! I used the anxiety and moved*
>   *ahead!*
> *Oh my God, I am* excited!

WORKAHOLISM

Workaholism is an addiction, and like all addictions, it blocks creative energy. In fact, it could be argued that the desire to block the fierce flow of creative energy is an underlying reason for addiction. If people are too busy to write morning pages, or too busy to take an artist date, they are probably too busy to hear the voice of authentic creative urges. To return to the concept of a radio set, the workaholic jams the signals with self-induced static.

Only recently recognized as an addiction, workaholism still receives a great deal of support in our society. The phrase *I'm working* has a certain unassailable air of goodness and duty to it. The truth is, we are very often working to avoid ourselves, our spouses, our real feelings.

In creative recovery, it is far easier to get people to do the extra work of the morning pages than it is to get them to do the assigned play of an artist date. Play can make a workaholic very nervous. Fun is scary.

"If I had more time, I'd have more fun," we like to tell ourselves, but this is seldom the truth. To test the validity of this assertion, ask yourself how much time you allot each week to fun: pure, unadulterated, nonproductive fun?

For most blocked creatives, fun is something they avoid almost as assiduously as their creativity. Why? Fun leads to creativity. It leads to rebellion. It leads to feeling our own power, and that is scary. "I may have a small problem with overwork," we like to tell ourselves, "but I am not really a workaholic." Try answering these questions before you are so sure:

The Workaholism Quiz

1. I work outside of office hours: seldom, often, never?

2. I cancel dates with loved ones to do more work: seldom, often, never?

3. I postpone outings until the deadline is over: seldom, often, never?

4. I take work with me on weekends: seldom, often, never?

5. I take work with me on vacations: seldom, often, never?

6. I take vacations: seldom, often, never?

7. My intimates complain I always work: seldom, often, never?

8. I try to do two things at once: seldom, often, never?

9. I allow myself free time between projects: seldom, often, never?

10. I allow myself to achieve closure on tasks: seldom, often, never?

11. I procrastinate in finishing up the last loose ends: seldom, often, never?

12. I set out to do one job and start on three more at the same time: seldom, often, never?

13. I work in the evenings during family time: seldom, often, never?

14. I allow calls to interrupt—and lengthen—my work day: seldom, often, never?

15. I prioritize my day to include an hour of creative work/play: seldom, often, never?

16. I place my creative dreams before my work: seldom, often, never?

When we are really honest with ourselves we must admit our lives are all that really belong to us. So it is how we use our lives that determines the kind of men we are.

CESAR CHAVEZ

17. I fall in with others' plans and fill my free time with their agendas: seldom, often, never?

18. I allow myself down time to do *nothing:* seldom, often, never?

19. I use the word *deadline* to describe and rationalize my work load: seldom, often, never?

20. Going somewhere, even to dinner, with a notebook or my work numbers is something I do: seldom, often, never?

In order to recover our creativity, we must learn to see workaholism as a block instead of a building block. Work abuse creates in our artist a Cinderella Complex. We are always dreaming of the ball and always experiencing the ball and chain.

There is a difference between zestful work toward a cherished goal and workaholism. That difference lies less in the hours than it does in the emotional quality of the hours spent. There is a treadmill quality to workaholism. We depend on our addiction and we resent it. For a workaholic, work is synonymous with worth, and so we are hesitant to jettison any part of it.

In striving to clear the way for our creative flow, we must look at our work habits very clearly. We may not think we overwork until we look at the hours we put in. We may think our work is normal until we compare it with a normal forty-hour week.

One way to achieve clarity about our time expenditures is to keep a daily checklist and record of our time spent. Even an hour of creative work/play can go a long way toward offsetting the sense of workaholic desperation that keeps our dreams at bay.

Because workaholism is a process addiction (an addiction to a behavior rather than a substance), it is difficult to tell when we are indulging in it. An alcoholic gets sober by abstaining from alcohol. A workaholic gets sober by abstaining from *over*work. The trick is to define overwork—and this is where we often lie to ourselves, bargaining to hold on to those abusive behaviors that still serve us.

In order to guard against rationalization, it is very useful to set a *bottom line*. Each person's bottom line is different but should specifically mention those behaviors known to be off-limits. These specific behaviors make for more immediate recovery than a vague, generic resolve to do better.

If you really have no time, you need to make some room. It is more likely, however, that you have the time and are misspending it. Your time log will help you find those areas where you need to create boundaries. *Boundary* is another way to say bottom line.) "Bottom line, I will not _____." That is your boundary. See Setting a Bottom Line in this week's list of tasks.)

As with creative U-turns, recovery from workaholism may require that we enlist the help of our friends. Tell them what you are trying to accomplish. Ask them to remind you gently when you have strayed off your self-care course. (This will backfire if you enlist the help of people who are active workaholics themselves or who are so controlling that they will overcontrol you.) Bear in mind, however, that this is *your* problem. No one can police you into recovery. But in some parts of the country Workaholics Anonymous meetings are springing up, and these may help you enormously.

One very simple but effective way to check your own recovery progress is to post a sign in your work area. Also post this sign wherever you will read it: one on the bathroom mirror and one on the refrigerator, one on the nightstand, one in the car. . . . The sign reads: WORKAHOLISM IS A BLOCK, NOT A BUILDING BLOCK.

The life which is not examined is not worth living.

PLATO

DROUGHT

In any creative life there are dry seasons. These droughts appear from nowhere and stretch to the horizon like a Death Valley vista. Life loses its sweetness; our work feels mechanical, empty, forced. We feel we have nothing to say, and we are tempted to say nothing. These are the times when the morning pages are most difficult and most valuable.

Sell your cleverness and buy bewilderment.

JALAL UD-DIN RUMI

During a drought, the mere act of showing up on the page, like the act of walking through a trackless desert, requires one footfall after another to no apparent point. Doubts sidle up to us like sidewinders. "What's the use?" they hiss. Or "What do you expect?" Droughts tell us that they will last forever—and that we will not. A haunting anticipation of our own death, approaching long before we're ready for it, long before we've done anything of value, shimmers ahead of us like a ghastly mirage.

What do we do? We stumble on. How do we do that? We stay on the morning pages. This is not a rule for writers only. (The pages have nothing to do with writing, although they may facilitate it as they do all art forms.) For all creative beings, the morning pages are the lifeline—the trail we explore and the trail home to ourselves.

During a drought, the morning pages seem both painful and foolish. They feel like empty gestures—like making breakfast for the lover we know is leaving us anyhow. Hoping against hope that we will someday be creative again, we go through the motions. Our consciousness is parched. We cannot feel so much as a trickle of grace.

During a drought (during a *doubt,* I just accurately wrote with a slip of the finger), we are fighting with God. We have lost faith—in the Great Creator and in our creative selves. We have some bone to pick, and bones to pick are everywhere. This is the desert of the heart. Looking for a hopeful sign, all we see are the hulking remains of dreams that died along the path.

And yet we write our morning pages because we must.

During a drought, emotions are dried up. Like water, they may exist somewhere underneath, but we have no access to them. A drought is a tearless time of grief. We are between dreams. Too listless to even know our losses, we put one page after another, more from habit than hope.

And yet we write our morning pages because we must.

Droughts are terrible. Droughts hurt. Droughts are long, airless seasons of doubt that make us grow, give us compassion, and blossom as unexpectedly as the desert with sudden flowers.

Droughts do end.

Droughts end because we have kept writing our pages. They end because we have not collapsed to the floor of our despair and refused to move. We have doubted, yes, but we have stumbled on.

In a creative life, droughts are a necessity. The time in the *desert* brings us clarity and charity. When you are in a drought, know that it is to a purpose. And keep writing morning pages.

To write is to *right* things. Sooner or later—always later than we like—our pages will bring things right. A path will emerge. An insight will be a landmark that shows the way out of the wilderness. Dancer, sculptor, actor, painter, playwright, poet, performance artist, potter, artists all—the morning pages are both our wilderness and our trail.

FAME

Fame encourages us to believe that if it hasn't happened yet, it won't happen. Of course, *it* is fame. Fame is not the same as success, and in our true souls we know that. We know—and have felt—success at the end of a good day's work. But fame? It is addictive, and it always leaves us hungry.

Fame is a spiritual drug. It is often a by-product of our artistic work, but like nuclear waste, it can be a very dangerous by-product. Fame, the desire to attain it, the desire to hold on to it, can produce the "How am I doing?" syndrome. This question is not "Is the work going well?" This question is "How does it look to them?"

The point of the work *is* the work. Fame interferes with that perception. Instead of acting being about acting, it becomes about being a famous actor. Instead of writing being about writing, it becomes about being recognized, not just published.

We all like credit where credit is due. As artists, we don't always get it. Yet, focusing on fame—on whether we are getting enough—creates a continual feeling of lack. There is never enough of the fame drug. Wanting more will always snap at our heels, discredit our accomplishments, erode our joy at another's accomplishment.

Truly, it is in the darkness that one finds the light, so when we are in sorrow, then this light is nearest of all to us.

MEISTER ECKHART

The unconscious wants truth. It ceases to speak to those who want something else more than truth.

ADRIENNE RICH

(To test this, read any of the many fan magazines—*People,* for instance—and see if afterward your life somehow feels more shabby, less worthwhile. This is the fame drug at work.)

Remember, treating yourself like a precious object will make you strong. When you have been toxified by the fame drug, you need to detox by coddling yourself. What's in order here is a great deal of gentleness and some behavior that makes you like yourself. Sending postcards is a great trick. Mail one to yourself that says, "You are doing great . . ." It is very nice to get fan letters from ourselves.

In the long run, fan letters from ourselves—and our creative self—are what we are really after. Fame is really a shortcut for self-approval. Try approving of yourself just as you are— and spoiling yourself rotten with small kid's pleasures.

What we are really scared of is that without fame we won't be loved—as artists or as people. The solution to this fear is concrete, small, loving actions. We must actively, consciously, consistently, and creatively nurture our artist selves.

When the fame drug hits, go to your easel, your typewriter, your camera or clay. Pick up the tools of your work and begin to do just a little creative play.

Soon, very soon, the fame drug should start to lessen its hold. The only cure for the fame drug is creative endeavor. Only when we are being joyfully creative can we release the obsession with others and how they are doing.

COMPETITION

You pick up a magazine—or even your alumni news—and somebody, *somebody you know,* has gone further, faster, toward your dream. Instead of saying, "That proves it can be done," your fear will say, "He or she will succeed *instead* of me."

Competition is another spiritual drug. When we focus on competition we poison our own well, impede our own progress. When we are ogling the accomplishments of others, we take our eye away from our own through line. We ask ourselves the wrong questions, and those wrong questions give us the wrong answers.

"Why do I have such rotten luck? Why did he get his movie/article/play out before I got mine out? Is it because of sexism?" "What's the use? What do I have to offer?" We often ask these questions as we try to talk ourselves out of creating.

Questions like these allow us to ignore more useful questions: "Did I work on my play today? Did I make the deadline to mail it off where it needed to go? Have I done any networking on its behalf?"

These are the real questions, and focusing on them can be hard for us. No wonder it is tempting to take the first emotional drink instead. No wonder so many of us read *People* magazine (or the *New York Times Book Review,* or *Lears,* or *Mirabella,* or *Esquire*) and use them to wallow in a lot of unhealthy envy.

We make excuses for our avoidance, excuses focused on others. "Somebody (else) has probably said it, done it, thought it . . . and better. . . . Besides, they had connections, a rich father, they belong to a sought-after minority, they slept their way to the top . . ."

Competition lies at the root of much creative blockage. As artists, we must go within. We must attend to what it is our inner guidance is nudging us toward. We cannot afford to worry about what is in or out. If it is too early or late for a piece of work, its time will come again.

As artists, we cannot afford to think about who is getting ahead of us and how they don't deserve it. The desire to *be better than* can choke off the simple desire to *be.* As artists we cannot afford this thinking. It leads us away from our own voices and choices and into a defensive game that centers outside of ourselves and our sphere of influence. It asks us to define our own creativity in terms of someone else's.

This compare-and-contrast school of thinking may have its place for critics, but not for artists in the act of creation. Let the critics spot trends. Let reviewers concern themselves with what is in and what is not. Let us concern ourselves first and foremost with what it is within us that is struggling to be born.

When we compete with others, when we focus our creative concerns on the marketplace, we are really jostling with other artists in a creative footrace. This is the sprint mentality.

Only when he no longer knows what he is doing does the painter do good things.

EDGAR DEGAS

Looking for the short-term win, ignoring the long-term gain, we short-circuit the possibility of a creative life led by our own lights, not the klieg lights of fashion.

Whenever you are angered about someone else beating you out, remember this: the footrace mentality is *always* the ego's demand to be not just good but also first and best. It is the ego's demand that our work be totally original—as if such a thing were possible. All work is influenced by other work. All people are influenced by other people. No man is an island and no piece of art is a continent unto itself.

When we respond to art we are responding to its resonance in terms of our own experience. We seldom see anew in the sense of finding something utterly unfamiliar. Instead, we see *an old* in a new light.

If the demand to be original still troubles you, remember this: each of us is our own country, an interesting place to visit. It is the accurate mapping out of our own creative interests that invites the term *original*. We are the *origin* of our art, its homeland. Viewed this way, originality is the process of remaining true to ourselves.

The spirit of competition—as opposed to the spirit of creation—often urges us to quickly winnow out whatever doesn't seem like a winning idea. This can be very dangerous. It can interfere with our ability to carry a project to term.

A competitive focus encourages snap judgments: thumbs up or thumbs down. Does this project deserve to live? (No, our ego will say if it is looking for the fail-safe, surefire project that is a winner at a glance and for good.) Many hits are sure things only in retrospect. Until we know better, we call a great many creative swans ugly ducklings. This is an indignity we offer our brainchildren as they rear their heads in our consciousness. We judge them like beauty-pageant contestants. In a glance we may cut them down. We forget that not all babies are born beautiful, and so we abort the lives of awkward or unseemly projects that may be our finest work, out best creative ugly ducklings. An act of art needs time to mature. Judged early, it may be judged incorrectly.

Never, ever, judge a fledgling piece of work too quickly.

Be willing to paint or write badly while your ego yelps resistance. Your bad writing may be the syntactical breakdown necessary for a shift in your style. Your lousy painting may be pointing you in a new direction. Art needs time to incubate, to sprawl a little, to be ungainly and misshapen and finally emerge as itself. The ego hates this fact. The ego wants instant gratification and the addictive hit of an acknowledged win.

The need to win—now!—is a need to win approval from others. As an antidote, we must learn to approve of ourselves. Showing up for the work is the win that matters.

He who knows others is wise; he who knows himself is enlightened.

LAO-TZU

I will tell you what I have learned myself. For me, a long five or six mile walk helps. And one must go alone and every day.

BRENDA UELAND

TASKS ✉

1. The Deadlies: Take a piece of paper and cut seven small strips from it. On each strip write one of the following words: *alcohol, drugs, sex, work, money, food, family/friends.* Fold these strips of paper and place them in an envelope. We call these folded slips *the deadlies.* You'll see why in a minute. Now draw one of the deadlies from the envelope and write five ways in which it has had a negative impact on your life. (If the one you choose seems difficult or inapplicable to you, consider this resistance.) You will do this seven times, each time putting back the previous slip of paper so that you are always drawing from seven possible choices. Yes, you may draw the same deadly repeatedly. Yes, this is significant. Very often, it is the last impact on the final list of an annoying "Oh no, not again" that yields a break, through denial, into clarity.

2. Touchstones: Make a quick list of things you love, happiness touchstones for you. River rocks worn smooth, willow trees, cornflowers, chicory, real Italian bread, homemade vegetable soup, the Bo Deans' music, black beans and rice, the smell of new-mown grass, blue velvet (the cloth and the song), Aunt Minnie's crumb pie . . .

How often—even before we began—have we declared a task "impossible"? And how often have we construed a picture of ourselves as being inadequate? . . . A great deal depends upon the thought patterns we choose and on the persistence with which we affirm them.

PIERO FERRUCCI

Post this list where it can console you and remind you of your own personal touchstones. You may want to draw one of the items on your list—or acquire it. If you love blue velvet, get a remnant and use it as a runner on a sideboard or dresser, or tack it to the wall and mount images on it. Play a little.

3. The Awful Truth: Answer the following questions.

Tell the truth. What habit do you have that gets in the way of your creativity?

Tell the truth. What do you think might be a problem? It is.

What do you plan to do about the habit or problem?

What is your payoff in holding on to this block?

If you can't figure out your payoff, ask a trusted friend.

Tell the truth. Which friends make you doubt yourself? (The self-doubt is yours already, but they trigger it.)

Tell the truth. Which friends believe in you and your talent? (The talent is yours, but they make you feel it.)

What is the payoff in keeping your destructive friends? If the answer is, "I like them," the next question is, "Why?"

Which destructive habits do your destructive friends share with your destructive self?

Which constructive habits do your constructive friends share with your constructive self?

4. Setting a Bottom Line: Working with your answers to the questions above, try setting a bottom line for yourself. Begin with five of your most painful behaviors. You can always add more later.

- If you notice that your evenings are typically gobbled by your boss's extra assignments, then a rule must come into play: no work after six.

• If you wake at six and could write for an hour if you were not interrupted to look for socks and make breakfast and do ironing, the rules might be "No interrupting Mommy before 7:00 A.M."

• If you are working too many jobs and too many hours, you may need to look at your billing. Are you pricing yourself appropriately? Do some footwork. What are others in your field receiving? Raise your prices and lower your work load.

It's a funny thing about life; if you refuse to accept anything but the best, you very often get it.

SOMERSET MAUGHAM

Bottom Line

1. I will no longer work weekends.

2. I will no longer bring work with me on social occasions.

3. I will no longer place my work before my creative commitments. (No more canceling piano lessons or drawing class because of a sudden new deadline from my boss the workaholic.)

4. I will no longer postpone lovemaking to do latenight reading for work.

5. I will no longer accept business calls at home after six.

5. Cherishing:

1. List five small victories.

2. List three nurturing actions you took for your artist.

3. List three actions you could take to comfort your artist.

4. Make three nice promises to yourself. Keep them.

5. Do one lovely thing for yourself *each* day this week.

CHECK-IN ✐

1. How many days this week did you do your morning pages? Has reading your pages changed your writing? Are you still allowing yourself to write them freely?

2. Did you do your artist date this week? Let yourself do an extra one. What did you do? How did it feel?

3. Did you experience any synchronicity this week? What was it?

4. Were there any other issues this week that you consider significant for your recovery? Describe them.

Recovering a Sense of Autonomy

This week we focus on our artistic autonomy. We examine the ongoing ways in which we must nurture and accept ourselves as artists. We explore the behaviors that can strengthen our spiritual base and, therefore, our creative power. We take a special look at the ways in which success must be handled in order that we not sabotage our freedom.

ACCEPTANCE

I AM AN ARTIST. As an artist, I may need a different mix of stability and flow from other people. I may find that a nine-to-five job steadies me and leaves me freer to create. Or I may find that a nine-to-five drains me of energy and leaves me unable to create. I must experiment with what works for me.

An artist's cash flow is typically erratic. No law says we must be broke all the time, but the odds are good we may be broke some of the time. Good work will sometimes not sell. People will buy but not pay promptly. The market may be rotten even when the work is great. I cannot control these factors. Being true to the inner artist often results in work that sells—but not always. I have to free myself from determining my value and the value of my work by my work's market value.

The idea that money validates my credibility is very hard to shake. If money determines real art, then Gauguin was a charlatan. As an artist, I may never have a home that looks like *Town and Country*—or I may. On the other hand, I may have a book of poems, a song, a piece of performance art, a film.

I must learn that as an artist my credibility lies with me,

God, and my work. In other words, if I have a poem to write, I need to write that poem—whether it will sell or not.

I need to create what wants to be created. I cannot plan a career to unfold in a sensible direction dictated by cash flow and marketing strategies. Those things are fine; but too much attention to them can stifle the child within, who gets scared and angered when continually put off. Children, as we all know, do not deal well with "Later. Not now."

Since my artist is a child, the natural child within, I must make some concessions to its sense of timing. *Some* concessions does not mean total irresponsibility. What it means is letting the artist have quality time, knowing that if I let it do what it wants to it will cooperate with me in doing what I need to do.

Sometimes I will write badly, draw badly, paint badly, perform badly. I have a right to do that to get to the other side. Creativity is its own reward.

As an artist, I must be very careful to surround myself with people who nurture my artist—not people who try to overly domesticate it for my own good. Certain friendships will kick off my artistic imagination and others will deaden it.

I may be a good cook, a rotten housekeeper, and a strong artist. I am messy, disorganized except as pertains to writing, a demon for creative detail, and not real interested in details like polished shoes and floors.

To a large degree my life is my art, and when it gets dull, so does my work. As an artist, I may poke into what other people think of as dead ends: a punk band that I mysteriously fall for, a piece of gospel music that hooks my inner ear, a piece of red silk I just like and add to a nice outfit, thereby "ruining it."

As an artist, I may frizz my hair or wear weird clothes. I may spend too much money on perfume in a pretty blue bottle even though the perfume stinks because the bottle lets me write about Paris in the thirties.

As an artist, I write whether I think it's any good or not. I shoot movies other people may hate. I sketch bad sketches to say, "I was in this room. I was happy. It was May and I was meeting somebody I wanted to meet."

As an artist, my self-respect comes from doing the work. One performance at a time, one gig at a time, one painting at a

Art happens—no hovel is safe from it, no prince can depend on it, the vastest intelligence cannot bring it about.

JAMES ABBOTT
McNEILL WHISTLER

time. Two and a half years to make one 90-minute piece of film. Five drafts of one play. Two years working on a musical. Throughout it all, daily, I show up at the morning pages and I write about my ugly curtains, my rotten haircut, my delight in the way the light hit the trees on the morning run.

As an artist, I do not need to be rich but I do need to be richly supported. I cannot allow my emotional and intellectual life to stagnate or the work will show it. My life will show it. My temperament will show it. If I don't create, I get crabby.

As an artist, I can literally die from boredom. I kill myself when I fail to nurture my artist child because I am acting like somebody else's idea of an adult. The more I nurture my artist child, the more adult I am able to appear. Spoiling my artist means it will let me type a business letter. Ignoring my artist means a grinding depression.

There is a connection between self-nurturing and self-respect. If I allow myself to be bullied and cowed by other people's urges for me to be more normal or more nice, I sell myself out. They may like me better, feel more comfortable with my more conventional appearance or behavior, but I will hate myself. Hating myself, I may lash out at myself and others.

If I sabotage my artist, I can well expect an eating binge, a sex binge, a temper binge. Check the relationship between these behaviors for yourself. When we are not creating, artists are not always very normal or very nice—to ourselves or to others.

Creativity is oxygen for our souls. Cutting off our creativity makes us savage. We react like we are being choked. There is a real rage that surfaces when we are interfered with on a level that involves picking lint off of us and fixing us up. When well-meaning parents and friends push marriage or nine-to-five or anything on us that doesn't evolve in a way that allows for our art to continue, we will react as if we are fighting for our lives—we are.

To be an artist is to recognize the particular. To appreciate the peculiar. To allow a sense of play in your relationship to accepted standards. To ask the question "Why?" To be an artist is to risk admitting that much of what is money, property, and prestige strikes you as just a little silly.

The job of the artist is always to deepen the mystery.

FRANCIS BACON

The function of the creative artist consists of making laws, not in following laws already made.

FERRUCCIO BUSONI

To be an artist is to acknowledge the astonishing. It is to allow the wrong piece in a room if we like it. It is to hang on to a weird coat that makes us happy. It is to not keep trying to be something that we aren't.

If you are happier writing than not writing, painting than not painting, singing than not singing, acting than not acting, directing than not directing, for God's sake (and I mean that literally) let yourself do it.

To kill your dreams because they are irresponsible is to be irresponsible to yourself. Credibility lies with you and God—not with a vote of your friends and acquaintances.

The creator made us creative. Our creativity is our gift *from* God. Our use of it is our gift *to* God. Accepting this bargain is the beginning of true self-acceptance.

SUCCESS

Creativity is a spiritual practice. It is not something that can be perfected, finished, and set aside. It is my experience that we reach plateaus of creative attainment only to have a certain restlessness set in. Yes, we are successful. Yes, we have made it, but . . .

In other words, just when we get there, *there* disappears. Dissatisfied with our accomplishments, however lofty, we are once again confronted with our creative self and its hungers. The questions we have just laid to rest now rear their heads again: what are we going to do . . . *now?*

This unfinished quality, this restless appetite for further exploration, tests us. We are asked to expand in order that we not contract. Evading this commitment—an evasion that tempts us all—leads straight to stagnation, discontent, spiritual discomfort. "Can't I rest?" we wonder. In a word, the answer is no.

As artists, we are spiritual sharks. The ruthless truth is that if we don't keep moving, we sink to the bottom and die. The choice is very simple: we can insist on resting on our laurels, or we can begin anew. The stringent requirement of a sustained creative life is the humility to start again, to begin anew.

It is this willingness to once more be a beginner that dis-

What moves men of genius, or rather what inspires their work, is not new ideas, but their obsession with the idea that what has already been said is still not enough.

EUGÈNE DELACROIX

tinguishes a creative career. A friend of mine, a master in his field, finds himself uncomfortably committed years in advance of his availability. He is in an enviable position on a business level, but he finds it increasingly perilous to his artistic health. When the wheel turns and the project committed to three years ago must be executed, can he do it with imagination and his initial enthusiasm? The honest answer is often an uncomfortable *no*. And so, at great financial cost, he has begun cutting back his future commitments, investing in the riskier but more rewarding gain of artistic integrity.

No amount of skillful invention can replace the essential element of imagination.

Edward Hopper

Not all of us, always, can muster such creative courage in the face of fiscal temptation, but we can try. We can at least be willing. As artists, we are travelers. Too heavily encumbered by our worldly dignity, too invested in our stations and positions, we are unable to yield to our spiritual leadings. We insist on a straight and narrow when the Artist's Way is a spiral path. Invested in the outer trappings of a career, we can place that investment above our inner guidance. Deciding to play by the numbers, we lose our commitment to counting ourselves and our own goals worthy.

Creativity is not a business, although it may generate much business. An artist cannot replicate a prior success indefinitely. Those who attempt to work too long with formula, even their own formula, eventually leach themselves of their creative truths. Embedded as we often are in the business milieu of our art, it is tempting to guarantee what we cannot deliver: good work that duplicates the good work that has gone before.

Successful movies generate a business demand for sequels. Successful books generate a demand for further, similar books. Painters pass through popular periods in their work and may be urged to linger there. For potters, composers, choreographers, the problem is the same. As artists, we are asked to repeat ourselves and expand on the market we have built. Sometimes this is possible for us. Other times it's not.

As a successful artist, the trick is to not mortgage the future too heavily. If the house in the Hamptons costs two years of creative misery cranking out a promised project just for cash, that house is an expensive luxury.

You are lost the instant you know what the result will be.

JUAN GRIS

This is not to say that editors should stop planning seasons or that studios should scuttle their business bottom line. It *is* to say that the many creatives laboring in fiscal settings should remember to commit themselves not only to projects that smack of the sure thing but also to those riskier projects that call to their creative souls. You don't need to overturn a successful career in order to find creative fulfillment. It *is* necessary to overturn each day's schedule slightly to allow for those small adjustments in daily trajectory that, over the long haul, alter the course and the satisfactions of our careers.

This means writing your morning pages. Taking your artist date. "But I run a studio," you say—or whatever other thing it is you must do. "People depend on me." I say, all the more reason to depend on yourself and protect your own creativity.

If we ignore our inner commitment, the cost rapidly becomes apparent in the outer world. A certain lackluster tone, a rote inevitability, evicts creative excitement from our lives and, eventually, our finances. Attempting to insure our finances by playing it safe, we lose our cutting edge. As the promised projects diverge further and further from our inner leanings, a certain deep artistic weariness sets in. We must summon our enthusiasm at gunpoint instead of reveling in each day's creative task.

Artists can and do responsibly meet the demands of their business partnerships. What is more difficult and more critical is for us as artists to continue to meet the inner demand of our own artistic growth. In short, as success comes to us, we must be vigilant. Any success postulated on a permanent artistic plateau dooms us, and it, to failure.

THE ZEN OF SPORTS

Most blocked creatives are cerebral beings. We think of all the things we want to do but can't. Early in recovery, we next think of all the things we want to do but don't. In order to effect a real recovery, one that lasts, we need to move out of the head and into a body of work. To do this, we must first of all move *into the body.*

Again, this is a matter that requires acceptance. Creativity requires action, and part of that action must be physical. It is one of the pitfalls of Westerners adopting Eastern meditation techniques to bliss out and render ourselves high but dysfunctional. We lose our grounding and, with it, our capacity to act in the world. In the pursuit of higher consciousness, we render ourselves unconscious in a new way. Exercise combats this spiritually induced dysfunction.

No longer conscious of my movement, I discovered a new unity with nature. I had found a new source of power and beauty, a source I never dreamt existed.

ROGER BANNISTER
ON BREAKING THE
FOUR-MINUTE MILE

Returning to the notion of ourselves as spiritual radio sets, we need enough energy to raise a strong signal. This is where walking comes in. What we are after here is a *moving* meditation. This means one where the act of motion puts us into the now and helps us to stop spinning. Twenty minutes a day is sufficient. The object is to stretch your mind more than your body, so there doesn't need to be an emphasis on fitness, although eventual fitness is a likely result.

The goal is to connect to a world outside of us, to lose the obsessive self-focus of self-exploration and, simply, explore. One quickly notes that when the mind is focused on *other,* the self often comes into a far more accurate focus.

It is 6:30 A.M. when the great blue heron stirs from its resting place in the short grasses and rises above the river on huge rhythmic wings. The bird sees Jenny down below. Jenny, down below, sees the bird. The pumping of her legs carries her in an effortless floating stride. Her spirit soars up to the heron and chirps. "Hello, good morning, lovely, isn't it?" At this time, in this place, they are kindred spirits. Both are wild and free and happy in their motion, in the movement of the winds, the clouds, the trees.

It is 4:30 P.M. when Jenny's boss looms in the doorway to her office. The new account is being picky and wants still more changes in her copy. Can she handle that? "Yes," Jenny says. She can because she is still soaring on the glad energy of her morning's run. That heron; the steely blue of it flashing silver as it made that great banking turn . . .

Jenny would not call herself an athlete. She does not run in marathons. She does not run in cheery singles groups. Although her distances have gradually increased and her thighs have gradually decreased, she does not run for fitness. Jenny runs for her soul, not her body. It is the fitness of her spirit that sets the tone of her days, changes their timbre from strained to effortless.

"I run for perspective," says Jenny. When the client picks at her copy, Jenny detaches and soars above her frustration like the great blue heron. It is not that she doesn't care. It is that she has a new perspective—a bird's eye view— on the place of her tribulations in the universe.

Eve Babitz is a novelist—and a swimmer. Tall, blond, and as generously curved as the freeway cloverleaf of her native Los Angeles, Babitz swims in order to direct the traffic flow of her own overcrowded mind. "Swimming," she says, "is a wonderful sport for a writer." Every day, as she swims the aquamarine oblong of her neighborhood pool, her mind dives deep into itself, past the weeds and clutter of its everyday concerns—what editor is late with a check, why the typist persists in making so many errors—and down to a quiet green pool of inspiration. That rhythmic, repetitive action transfers the locus of the brain's energies from the logic to the artist hemisphere. It is there that inspiration bubbles up untrammeled by the constraints of logic.

Martha is a carpenter and a long-distance bicyclist. Carpentry challenges her daily to find innovative solutions to construction problems, to untangle the intricacies of a complicated design situation requiring a simple answer to a complicated question. "How can I build in work space without using floor space when I'm done working?" or "Is there some kind of cabinet that could fit in this corner and around on this wall without seeming too modern for my furniture?" Pedaling from her home in the suburbs to her job in the city, Martha encounters her answers to these questions. In much the same way that a red-winged blackbird will suddenly take flight and cross her line of vision, Martha will be pedaling when "louvered doors" will flash as a design solution. Pumping her bicycle rhythmically and repetitively, Martha also pumps the well of her creativity. "It is my time to let my imagination roam and work out problems," Martha says. "Solutions just come. Somehow I am freed to free-associate, and things begin to fall into place."

The things that begin to fall into place are not merely work associated. When she bicycles, Martha has a sense not only of her own motion but also of the motion of God through the universe. She remembers riding alone on Route 22 in upstate New York. The sky was an azure bowl. The cornfields were green and gold. The ribbon of black asphalt that Martha rode seemed to her to head straight into the heart of God. "Silence, a blue sky, a black ribbon of highway, God, and the wind. When I ride, especially at dusk and at early morning, I feel God. I am able to meditate more in motion than sitting still. Being alone, having the freedom to go wherever I want, having the wind blow, riding alone in that wind, allows me to center myself. I feel God so closely that my spirit sings."

Exercise teaches the rewards of process. It teaches the sense of satisfaction over small tasks well done. Jenny, running, extends herself and learns to tap into an unexpected inner resource. Martha would call that power *God,* but whatever it answers to, exercise seems to call it forth in other circumstances when we mistrust our personal strength. Rather than scotch a creative project when it frustrates us, we learn to move through the difficulty.

"Life *is* a series of hurdles," says Libby, a painter whose sport is horseback riding. "I used to see it as a series of obstacles or roadblocks. Now they are hurdles and challenges. How well am I taking them?" In the daily schooling of her horse, "teaching her to think before she jumps, to pace herself properly," Libby has learned the same skills for her own life.

Part of this learned creative patience has to do with connecting to a sense of universal creativity. "Riding, my rational mind switches off," she says. "I am reduced to feeling, to being a participant. When you ride through a field of grass and little flecks of fluff from the wheat ears float around you, the feeling makes your heart sing. When a rooster tail of snow sparkles in the sun in your wake, that makes your heart sing. These moments of intense feeling have taught me to be aware of other moments in my life as they occur. When I feel that singing feeling with a man and know that I have also felt it in a field of grass and a field of snow, then I know that is really my own capacity to feel that I am celebrating."

It is not only the sense of a communion with nature that

Here in this body are the sacred rivers: here are the sun and moon as well as all the pilgrimage places. . . . I have not encountered another temple as blissful as my own body.

SARAHA

creates a singing in the heart. An endorphin-induced natural high is one of the by-products of exercise itself. A runner may feel the same celebratory sense of well-being pounding a dirty city street that Libby finds as she posts rhythmically along a country trail.

"God is in his heaven; all's right with the world" is how Robert Browning characterized this feeling in his long narrative poem *Pippa Passes.* It is no coincidence that Pippa experienced this feeling as she was walking. Not everyone can afford to ride a horse or even a ten-speed bicycle. Many of us must rely on our feet for transportation and for recreation. Like Jenny, we can take up running. Or we might make walking our sport. As an artist, walking offers the added benefit of sensory saturation. Things do not whiz by. We really see them. In a sense, insight follows from sight. We fill the well and later tap it more easily.

Gerry is a confirmed city dweller. His country walks are limited to perusing window boxes and pocket gardens. Gerry has learned that "in cities, people are the scenery." He has also learned to look up, not down, and to admire the frippery and friezes that often grace buildings that look quite, well, pedestrian at street level. As he roves the city canyons, Gerry has found a whole panoply of scenic attractions. There is the orange-marmalade cat that sits in the window above the window box with both pink and red geraniums. There is the copper church roof gone murky green that glistens silver in rainstorms. An ornately inlaid marble foyer can be glimpsed through the doors of one mid-town office building. On another block, someone has sunk a lucky horseshoe in civic concrete. A miniature Statue of Liberty soars unexpectedly atop a dignified brick facade. Gerry feels at liberty himself, roaming the city streets on tireless feet. This courtyard, that cobbled walkway—Gerry gathers urban visual delights the same way his primordial ancestors gathered this nut, that berry. They gathered food. He gathers food for thought. Exercise, much maligned as mindless activity among certain intellectuals, turns out to be thought-provoking instead.

As we said before, we learn by going where we have to go. Exercise is often the going that moves us from stagnation to inspiration, from problem to solution, from self-pity to self-respect. We *do* learn by going. We learn we are stronger than we thought. We learn to look at things with a new perspective. We learn to solve our problems by tapping our own inner resources and listening for inspiration, not only from others but from ourselves. Seemingly without effort, our answers come while we swim or stride or ride or run. By definition, this is one of the fruits of exercise: "*exercise:* the act of bringing into play or realizing in action" (*Webster's Ninth*).

God bless the roots! Body and soul are one.

THEODORE ROETHKE

BUILDING YOUR ARTIST'S ALTAR

Morning pages are meditation, a practice that bring you to your creativity and your creator God. In order to stay easily and happily creative, we need to stay spiritually centered. This is easier to do if we allow ourselves centering rituals. It is important that we devise these ourselves from the elements that feel holy and happy to us.

Many blocked creatives grew up in punitively religious homes. For us to stay happily and easily creative, we need to heal from this, becoming spiritually centered through creative rituals of our own. A spiritual room or even a spiritual corner is an excellent way to do this.

This haven can be a corner of a room, a nook under the stairs, even a window ledge. It is a reminder and an acknowledgment of the fact that our creator unfolds our creativity. Fill it with things that make you happy. Remember that your artist is fed by images. We need to unlearn our old notion that spirituality and sensuality don't mix. An artist's altar should be a sensory experience.

We are meant to celebrate the good things of this earth. Pretty leaves, rocks, candles, sea treasures—all these remind us of our creator.

Small rituals, self-devised, are good for the soul. Burning incense while reading affirmations or writing them, lighting a candle, dancing to drum music, holding a smooth rock and listening to Gregorian chant—all of these tactile, physical techniques reinforce spiritual growth.

Remember, the artist child speaks the language of the soul: music, dance, scent, shells . . . Your artist's altar to the creator should be fun to look at, even silly. Remember how much little kids like gaudy stuff. Your artist is a little kid, so . . .

Art does not reproduce the visible; rather, it makes it visible. The moon develops creativity as chemicals develop photographic images.

NORMA JEAN HARRIS

TASKS ✉

1. Tape your own voice reading the Basic Principles. (See page 3). Choose a favorite essay from this book and tape that as well. Use this tape for meditation.

2. Write out, in longhand, your Artist's Prayer from Week Four. Place it in your wallet.

3. Buy yourself a special creativity notebook. Number pages one through seven. Give one page each to the following categories: health, possessions, leisure, relationships, creativity, career, and spirituality. With no thought as to practicality, list ten wishes in each area. All right, it's a lot. Let yourself dream a little here.

4. Working with the Honest Changes section in Week Four, inventory for yourself the ways you have changed since beginning your recovery.

5. List five ways you will change as you continue.

6. List five ways you plan to nurture yourself in the next six months: courses you will take, supplies you will allow yourself, artist's dates, and vacations just for you.

7. Take out a piece of paper and plan one week's nurturing for yourself. This means one concrete, loving action every single day for one week: please binge!

8. Write and mail an encouraging letter to your inner artist. This sounds silly and feels very, very good to receive. Remember that your artist is a child and loves praise and encouragement and festive plans.

9. Once more, reexamine your God concept. Does your belief system limit or support your creative expansion? Are you open minded about altering your concept of God?

10. List ten examples of personal synchronicity that support the possibility of a nurturing creative force.

CHECK-IN ✐

1. How many days this week did you do your morning pages? How was the experience for you? Have you recommended morning pages to anyone else? Why?

2. Did you do your artist date this week? (Have you considered scheduling an entire artist's day? Whew!) What did you do? How did it feel?

3. Did you experience any synchronicity this week? What was it?

4. Were there any other issues this week that you consider significant for your recovery? Describe them.

Recovering a Sense of Faith

TRUSTING

Adventures don't begin until you get into the forest. That first step in an act of faith.

MICKEY HART
GRATEFUL DEAD DRUMMER

CREATIVITY REQUIRES FAITH. FAITH requires that we relinquish control. This is frightening, and we resist it. Our resistance to our creativity is a form of self-destruction. We throw up roadblocks on our own path. Why do we do this? In order to maintain an illusion of control. Depression, like anger and anxiety, is resistance, and it creates dis-ease. This manifests itself as sluggishness, confusion, "I don't know . . ."

The truth is, we do know and we *know* that we know.

Each of us has an inner dream that we can unfold if we will just have the courage to admit what it is. And the faith to trust our own admission. The admitting is often very difficult. A clearing affirmation can often open the channel. One excellent one is "I know the things I know." Another is "I trust my own inner guide." Either of these will eventually yield us a sense of our own direction—which we will often then promptly resist!

In this final week, we acknowledge the inherently mysterious spiritual heart of creativity. We address the fact that creativity requires receptivity and profound trust—capacities we have developed through our work in this course. We set our creative aims and take a special look at last-minute sabotage. We renew our commitment to the use of the tools.

Do not fear mistakes—there are none.

MILES DAVIS

This resistance is really very understandable. We are not accustomed to thinking that God's will for us and our own inner dreams can coincide. Instead, we have bought the message of our culture: this world is a vale of tears and we are meant to be dutiful and then die. The truth is that we are meant to be bountiful and *live*. The universe will always support affirmative action. Our truest dream for ourselves is always God's will for us.

Mickey Hart's hero and mentor, the late, great mythologist Joseph Campbell, wrote, "Follow your bliss and doors will open where there were no doors before." It is the inner commitment to be true to ourselves and follow our dreams that triggers the support of the universe. While we are ambivalent, the universe will seem to us also to be ambivalent and erratic. The flow through our lives will be characterized by spurts of abundance and long spells of drought, when our supply dwindles to a mere trickle.

If we look back at the times when the world seemed to be a capricious and untrustworthy place, we see that we were ourselves ambivalent and conflicted in our goals and behaviors. Once we trigger an internal yes by affirming our truest goals and desires, the universe mirrors that yes and expands it.

There is a path for each of us. When we are on our right path, we have a surefootedness. We know the next right action—although not necessarily what is just around the bend. By trusting, we *learn* to trust.

MYSTERY

Creativity—like human life itself—begins in darkness. We need to acknowledge this. All too often, we think only in terms of light: "And then the lightbulb went on and I got it!" It is true that insights may come to us as flashes. It is true that some of these flashes may be blinding. It is, however, also true that such bright ideas are preceded by a gestation period that is interior, murky, and completely necessary.

We speak often about ideas as brainchildren. What we do not realize is that brainchildren, like all babies, should not be dragged from the creative womb prematurely. Ideas, like sta-

lactites and stalagmites, form in the dark inner cave of consciousness. They form in drips and drops, not by squared-off
building blocks. We must learn to wait for an idea to hatch. Or,
to use a gardening image, we must learn to not pull our ideas
up by the roots to see if they are growing.

Mulling on the page is an artless art form. It is fooling
around. It is doodling. It is the way that ideas slowly take shape
and form until they are ready to help us see the light. All too
often, we try to push, pull, outline, and control our ideas instead of letting them grow organically. The creative process is
a process of surrender, not control.

Mystery is at the heart of creativity. That, and surprise. All
too often, when we say we want to be creative, we mean that
we want to be able to be productive. Now, to be creative *is* to be
productive—but by cooperating with the creative process, not
forcing it.

As creative channels, we need to trust the darkness. We
need to learn to gently mull instead of churning away like a little engine on a straight-ahead path. This mulling on the page
can be very threatening. "I'll never get any *real* ideas this way!"
we fret.

Hatching an idea is a lot like baking bread. An idea needs
to rise. If you poke at it too much at the beginning, if you keep
checking on it, it will never rise. A loaf of bread or a cake, baking, must stay for a good long time in the darkness and safety
of the oven. Open that oven too soon and the bread col-
lapses—or the cake gets a hole in its middle because all the
steam has rushed out of it. Creativity requires a respectful reti-
cence.

The truth is that this is how to raise the best ideas. Let them
grow in dark and mystery. Let them form on the roof of our
consciousness. Let them hit the page in droplets. Trusting this
slow and seemingly random drip, we will be startled one day
by the flash of "Oh! That's *it!*"

THE IMAGINATION AT PLAY

When we think about creativity, it is all too easy to think *art*
with a capital *A*. For our purposes, capital-*A* art is a scarlet

*The most beautiful thing we can
experience is the mysterious.*

ALBERT EINSTEIN

*What shakes the eye but the
invisible?*

THEODORE ROETHKE

letter, branding us as doomed. In order to nurture our creativity, we require a sense of festivity, even humor: "Art. That's somebody my sister used to date."

We are an ambitious society, and it is often difficult for us to cultivate forms of creativity that do not directly serve us and our career goals. Recovery urges our reexamining definitions of creativity and expanding them to include what in the past we called hobbies. The experience of creative living argues that hobbies are in fact essential to the joyful life.

Then, too, there is the hidden benefit that they are also creatively useful. Many hobbies involve a form of artist-brain mulling that leads to enormous creative breakthroughs. When I have screenwriting students stuck at the midpoint of act two, I ask them to please go do their household mending. They usually balk, offended by such a mundane task, but sewing has a nice way of mending up plots. Gardening is another hobby I often assign to creativity students. When someone is panicked halfway across the bridge into a new life, repotting plants into larger and better containers quite literally grounds that person and gives him or her a sense of expansion.

Spiritual benefits accompany the practice of a hobby. There is a release into humility that comes from doing something by rote. As we serve our hobby, we are freed from our ego's demands and allowed the experience of merging with a greater source. This conscious contact frequently affords us the perspectives needed to solve vexing personal or creative conundrums.

It is a paradox of creative recovery that we must get serious about taking ourselves lightly. We must work at learning to play. Creativity must be freed from the narrow parameters of capital *A* art and recognized as having much broader play (that word again).

As we work with our morning pages and artist dates, many forgotten samplings of our own creativity may come to mind.

- I had forgotten all about those paintings I did in high school. I loved painting those flats in drama tech!

- I suddenly remembered I played Antigone—who could forget her? I don't know if I was any good, but I remember I loved it.

- I'd forgotten all about the skits I wrote when I was ten. I set them all to Ravel's *Bolero* no matter what they were about. I made my brothers and sisters swoon about the living room.

- I used to tap-dance. I know you can't believe it now, but I was something!

As we write, digging ourselves out of denial, our memories, dreams, and creative plans all move to the surface. We discover anew that we are creative beings. The impulse cooks in us all, simmering along all the time—without our knowledge, without our encouragement, even without our approval. It moves beneath the surface of our lives, showing in bright flashes, like a penny, in our stream of thought—like new grass under snow.

We are intended to create. We refurbish a dowdy kitchen, tie bows on a holiday cat, experiment with a better soup. The same child who brewed perfume from a dab of this and a dash of that, half dish soap and part cinnamon, grows up to buy potpourri and to boil a spice pot that says, "Christmas."

As gray, as controlled, as dreamless as we may strive to be, the fire of our dreams will not stay buried. The embers are always there, stirring in our frozen souls like winter leaves. They won't go away. They are sneaky. We make a crazy doodle in a boring meeting. We post a silly card on our office board. We nickname the boss something wicked. Plant twice as many flowers as we need.

Restive in our lives, we yearn for more, we wish, we chafe. We sing in the car, slam down the phone, make lists, clear closets, sort through shelves. We want to do something but we think it needs to be the *right something,* by which we mean *something important.*

We are what's important, and the something that we do can be something festive but small: dead plants go; mismatched

For me a painting is like a story which stimulates the imagination and draws the mind into a place filled with expectation, excitement, wonder and pleasure.

J. P. HUGHSTON
PAINTER

Play is the exultation of
the possible.

MARTIN BUBER

socks bite the dust. We are stung by loss, bitten by hope. Working with our morning pages, a new—and gaudy?—life takes form. Who bought that azalea? Why the sudden taste for pink? Is this picture you've tacked up a *you* you're going toward?

Your shoes feel worn. You throw them out. There's a garage sale coming and you are playing host. You buy a first edition, splurge on new sheets. A friend worries once too often about what's come over you and you take your first vacation in years.

The clock is ticking and you're hearing the beat. You stop by a museum shop, sign your name on a scuba-diving sheet, and commit yourself to Saturday mornings in the deep end.

You're either losing your mind—or gaining your soul. Life is meant to be an artist date. That's why we were created.

ESCAPE VELOCITY

My friend Michele has a theory, a theory born of long and entangled romantic experience. In a nutshell, it goes: "When you're going to leave them, *they know.*"

This same theory applies to creative recovery. It occurs when you reach what Michele calls *escape velocity.* As she puts it, "There's this time for blast-off, like a NASA space launch, and you're heading for it when *wham,* you draw to you the Test."

"The Test?"

"Yeah. The Test. It's like when you're all set to marry the nice guy, the one who treats you right, and Mr. Poison gets wind of it and phones you up."

"Ah."

"The whole trick is to evade the Test. We all draw to us the one test that's our total nemesis."

A lawyer by trade and a writer by avocation and temperament, Michele is fond of conspiracy theories, which she lays out in sinister detail.

"Think of it. You're all set to go to the Coast on an important business trip, and your husband suddenly needs you, capital *N,* for no real reason. . . . You're all set to leave the bad job, and the boss from hell suddenly gives you your first raise in five years. . . . Don't be fooled. Don't be fooled."

Listening to Michele talk, it was clear that her years as a trial attorney stood her in good stead as a creative person. She, at least, was no longer fooled. But is it really so sinister as she implied? Do we really draw to us a Test? I thought about everything Michele had told me and I concluded that the answer was yes.

I thought of all the times I'd been fooled. There was the agent who managed to undo done deals but apologized so prettily. . . . There was the editor who asked for rewrite upon rewrite until gruel was all that remained, but who always said I wrote brilliantly and was her brightest star.

A little flattery can go a long way toward deterring our escape velocity. So can a little cash. More sinister than either is the impact a well-placed doubt can have, particularly a "for your own good, just wanting to make sure you've thought about this" doubt—voiced by one of our nearest and dearest.

As recovering creatives, many of us find that every time our career heats up we reach for our nearest Wet Blanket. We blurt out our enthusiasm to our most skeptical friend—in fact, we call him up. If we don't, he calls us. This is the Test.

Our artist is a child, an inner youngster, and when he/she is scared, Mommy is what's called for. Unfortunately, many of us have Wet Blanket mommies and a whole army of Wet Blanket surrogate mommies—those friends who have our second, third, and fourth thoughts for us. The trick is not to let them be that way. How? *Zip the lip. Button up. Keep a lid on it. Don't give away the gold.* Always remember: the first rule of magic is self-containment. You must hold your intention within yourself, stoking it with power. Only then will you be able to manifest what you desire.

In order to achieve escape velocity, we must learn to keep our own counsel, to move silently among doubters, to voice our plans only among our allies, and to name our allies accurately.

Make a list: those friends who will support me. Make another list: those friends who won't. Name your W. B.'s for what they are—Wet Blankets. Wrap yourself in something else—

One does not discover new lands without consenting to lose sight of the shore for a very long time.

ANDRÉ GIDE

dry ones. Fluffy heated towels. Do not indulge or tolerate *any-one* who throws cold water in your direction. Forget good intentions. Forget they didn't mean it. Remember to count your blessings and your toes. Escape velocity requires the sword of steely intention and the shield of self-determination.

"They will try to get you. Don't forget that," warns Michele. "Set your goals and set your boundaries."

I would add, set your sights and don't let the ogre that looms on the horizon deflect your flight.

TASKS ✉

1. Write down any resistance, angers, and fears you have about going on from here. We all have them.

2. Take a look at your current areas of procrastination. What are the payoffs in your waiting? Locate the hidden fears. Do a list on paper.

3. Sneak a peek at Week One, Core Negative Beliefs (see page 30.) Laugh. Yes, the nasty critters are still there. Note your progress. Read yourself the affirmations on pages 36 and 37. Write some affirmations about your continued creativity as you end the course.

4. Mend any mending.

5. Repot any pinched and languishing plants.

6. Select a God jar. A what? A jar, a box, a vase, a container. Something to put your fears, your resentments, your hopes, your dreams, your worries into.

7. Use your God jar. Start with your fear list from Task 1 above. When worried, remind yourself it's in the jar—"God's got it." Then take the next action.

8. *Now,* check *how*: Honestly, what would you most like to create? Open-minded, what oddball paths

would you dare to try? *Willing,* what appearances are you willing to shed to pursue your dream?

9. List five people you can talk to about your dreams and with whom you feel supported to dream and then plan.

10. Reread this book. Share it with a friend. Remember that the miracle is one artist sharing with another. Trust God. Trust yourself.

Good luck and God bless you!

CHECK-IN 🖉

1. How many days this week did you do your morning pages? Have you accepted them yet as a permanent spiritual practice? How was the experience for you?

2. Did you do your artist date this week? Will you allow yourself these on a permanent basis as well? What did you do? How did it feel?

3. Did you experience any synchronicity this week? What was it?

4. Were there any other issues this week that you consider significant for your recovery? Describe them.

As a recovering creative, you now have put many hours into your recovery over these three months, changing rapidly as you grew. For your recovery to continue, you require a commitment to further creative plans. The contract on the following page will help you accomplish them.

CREATIVITY CONTRACT

My name is _____. I am a recovering creative person. To further my growth and my joy, I now commit myself to the following self-nurturing plans:

Morning pages have been an important part of my self-nurturing and self-discovery. I, _____, hereby commit myself to continuing to work with them for the next ninety days.

Artist's dates have been integral to my growth in self-love and my deepening joy in living. I, _____, am willing to commit to another ninety days of weekly artist's dates for self-care.

In the course of following the *artist's way* and healing my artist within, I have discovered that I have a number of creative interests. While I hope to develop many of them, my specific commitment for the next ninety days is to allow myself to more fully explore _____.

My concrete commitment to a plan of action is a critical part of nurturing my artist. For the next ninety days, my planned, self-nurturing creative action plan is _____.

I have chosen _____ as my creative colleague and _____ as my creative back-up. I am committed to a weekly phone check-in.

I have made the above commitments and will begin my new commitment on _____.

_____   _____
(signature)   (date)

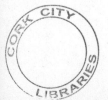

EPILOGUE

THE ARTIST'S WAY

IN ENDING THIS BOOK, I yearned for a final flourish, some last fillip of the imagination that would sign the book. This was a small and harmless conceit, I felt—until I remembered the number of times I have enjoyed a painting and been distracted by the outsized artistic signature of its maker. So, no final flourishes here.

The truth is that this book should probably end with an image from another book. As I recall it, and this may be my imagination and not my memory at work, an early edition of Thomas Merton's *Seven Story Mountain* featured a mountain on its book jacket—the seven-story mountain, no doubt.

Maybe it did and maybe it didn't. I read the book many years ago, a precocious twelve-year-old. What I conjure now is a mountain of Himalayan proportions with a path winding upward to its height. That path, a spiral path, is how I think of the Artist's Way. As we pursue climbing it, we circle back on the same views, over and over, at slightly different altitudes. "I've been here before," we think, hitting a spell of drought. And, in a sense, we have been. The road is never straight. Growth is a spiral process, doubling back on itself, reassessing and regrouping. As artists, our progress is often dogged by rough terrain or storms. A fog may obscure the distance we have covered or the progress we have made toward our goal. While the occasional dazzling vista may grace us, it is really best to proceed a step at a time, focusing on the path beneath our feet as much as the heights still before us.

The Artist's Way is a spiritual journey, a pilgrimage home to the self. Like all great journeys it entails dangers of the trail, some of which I have tried to enumerate in this book. Like all pilgrims, those of us on the Artist's Way will often be graced by fellow travelers and invisible companions. What I call my marching orders others may sense in themselves as a still, small voice or, even more simply, a hunch. The point is that you will hear something if you listen for it. Keep your soul cocked for guidance.

I finally discovered the source of all movement, the unity from which all diversities of movement are born.

ISADORA DUNCAN

Creation is only the projection into form of that which already exists.

SHRIMAD
BHAGAVATAM

When Mark Bryan began cornering me into writing this book, he had just seen a Chinese film about Tibet called *The Horse Thief*. It was an indelible film for him, a classic of the Beijing school, a film we have since searched for in Chinese video stores and film archives, to no avail. Mark told me about the film's central image: another mountain, a prayerful journey up that mountain, on bended knee: step, lie prostrate, stand and straighten, another step, lie prostrate . . .

In the film, this journey was the reparation that a thief and his wife had to make for damaging their society by dishonoring themselves through thievery. I have wondered, since then, if the mountain that I see when thinking of the Artist's Way isn't another mountain best climbed in the spirit of reparation—not to others, but to ourselves.

A painting is never finished—it simply stops in interesting places.

PAUL GARDNER

WORDS FOR IT

I wish I could take language
And fold it like cool, moist rags.
I would lay words on your forehead.
I would wrap words on your wrists.
"There, there," my words would say—
Or something better.
I would ask them to murmur,
"Hush" and "Shh, shhh, it's all right."
I would ask them to hold you all night.
I wish I could take language
And daub and soothe and cool
Where fever blisters and burns,
Where fever turns yourself against you.
I wish I could take language
And heal the words that were the wounds
You have no names for.

J.C.

FORMING A SACRED CIRCLE

When I was a little kid, one of my favorite heroes was Johnny Appleseed. I loved the idea of a vagrant wanderer traveling America, apple blossoms in his wake. It is my hope that this book will also create blossoming, that artists and circles of artists will spring into being. Trusting this to be the case, the following essay is intended for use in establishing your own artists' circle. It is my experience as a teacher that an atmosphere of safety and trust is critical to creative growth. I have found these guidelines to be helpful in establishing that atmosphere.

The Sacred Circle

Art is an act of the soul, not the intellect. When we are dealing with peoples' dreams—their visions, really—we are in the realm of the sacred. We are involved with forces and energies larger than our own. We are engaged in a sacred transaction of which we know only a little: the shadow, not the shape.

For these reasons, it is mandatory that any gathering of artists be in the spirit of a sacred trust. We invoke the Great Creator when we invoke our own creativity, and that creative force has the power to alter lives, fulfill destinies, answer our dreams.

In our human lives, we are often impatient, ill-tempered, inappropriate. We find it difficult to treat our intimates with the love we really hold for them. Despite this, they bear with us because of the larger, higher level of family that they honor even in our outbursts. This is their commitment.

As artists, we belong to an ancient and holy tribe. We are the carriers of the truth that spirit moves through us all. When we deal with one another, we are dealing not merely with our human personalities but also with the unseen but ever-present throng of ideas, visions, stories, poems, songs, sculptures, art-as-facts that crowd the temple of consciousness waiting their turn to be born.

We are meant to midwife dreams for one another. We cannot labor in place of one another, but we can support the labor that each must undertake to birth his or her art and foster it to maturity.

It is for all these reasons that the Sacred Circle must exist in any place of creation. It is this protective ring, this soul boundary, that enlivens us at our highest level. By drawing and acknowledging the Sacred Circle, we declare principles to be above personalities. We invite a spirit of service to the highest good and a faith in the accomplishment of our own good in the midst of our fellows.

Envy, backbiting, criticism have no place in our midst, nor do ill temper, hostility, sarcasm, chivvying for position. These attitudes may belong in the world, but they do not belong among us in our place as artists.

Success occurs in clusters. Drawing a Sacred Circle creates a sphere of safety and a center of attraction for our good. By filling this form faithfully, we draw to us the best. We draw the people we need. We attract the gifts we could best employ.

The Sacred Circle is built on respect and trust. The image is of the garden. Each plant has its name and its place. There is no one flower that cancels the need for another. Each bloom has its unique and irreplaceable beauty.

Let our gardening hands be gentle ones. Let us not root up one another's ideas before they have time to bloom. Let us bear with the process of growth, dormancy, cyclicality, fruition, and reseeding. Let us never be hasty to judge, reckless in our urgency to force unnatural growth. Let there be, always, a place for the artist toddler to try, to falter, to fail, to try again. Let us remember that in nature's world every loss has meaning. The same is true for us. Turned to good use, a creative failure may be the compost that nourishes next season's creative success. Remember, we are in this for the long haul, the ripening and harvest, not the quick fix.

Art is an act of the soul: ours is a spiritual community.

I have been a working artist for twenty-five years and for the past fifteen I have taught creative recovery. In that time, I have had ample opportunity to experience first hand what it means to lack creative support and what it means to find it.

God is glorified in the fruitage of our lives.

JOEL S. GOLDSMITH

Often, it is the difference between success and failure, between hope and despair.

What we are talking about here is the power of breaking isolation. As in any other recovery process, this act is a potent first step. Creative recovery, like any other recovery, may be facilitated by the company of like-minded people. For recovery from something, Twelve Steps groups seem to work especially well. For recovery to something, Creative Clusters show remarkable results.

When people ask me what I think is the single most important factor in an artist's sustained productivity, I know I am supposed to say something like, "Solitude", or "An independent income", or "Childcare". All of these things are good and many people have said so, but what I think is better and more important than any of these things is what I call "a believing mirror".

Put simply, a believing mirror is a friend to your creativity—someone who believes in you and your creativity. As artists, we can consciously build what I call Creative Clusters—a Sacred Circle of believing mirrors to potentiate each other's growth, to mirror a "yes" to each other's creativity.

In my experience we can benefit greatly from the support of others who share our dreams of living a fuller life. I suggest forming a weekly cluster and going through the exercises in the book together, sharing and comparing each answer. Often someone else's breakthrough insight can trigger one of our own.

Remember, we live in a culture that is toxic to art. A remarkable number of toxic myths about artists flourish. In addition to our purportedly being broke, irresponsible, drug-riddled and crazy, artists are also deemed selfish, out of touch with reality, megalomaniacs, tyrants, depressives and, above all, people who "want to be left alone".

At the very least, we are sure we will be.

Ask budding artists why they are afraid to move deeply into their creativity and they will tell you, "I'm not sure I want to spend the rest of my life alone."

In America, we seem to confuse artists with cowboys. We see artists as self-contained, driven loners who are always riding off into the sunset to do our thing—alone. If you'll pardon the joke, the cowboy analogy is so much bull. Most of us enjoy a little company. One of our great cultural secrets is the fact that artists like other artists.

Think about it for just a second: what did the Impressionists paint? Lunch . . . with each other. What did the Bloomsbury Group write about? Dining out with—and gossiping about—each other. Who did John Cassavetes make films with? His friends. Why? Because they believed in each other and enjoyed helping each other realize their dreams.

Artists like other artists. We are not supposed to know this. We are encouraged to believe "there is only so much room at the top". Hooey. Water seeks its own level and water rises collectively.

Artists often help each other. We always have, although mythology tells us otherwise. The truth is that when we do, very powerful things happen. I will give a case in point. Film director Martin Scorsese developed, shaped and fine-tuned the script for *Schindler's List*—then gave the project to his friend Steven Spielberg, feeling the material should be his. This unballyhooed act of creative generosity finally gave Spielberg his shot at an Oscar as "a real director"—even though Scorsese knew it might cost him his own shot, at least this year. And yet, to read about it in the press, these men are pitted against each other, artist versus artist, like athletes from warring nations in our mini-wars, the Olympics. Hooey, again.

Success occurs in clusters.

As artists, we must find those who believe in us, and in whom we believe, and band together for support, encouragement and protection.

I remember sitting in a hotel room twenty years ago with two then-little-known directors Brian De Palma and Steven Spielberg. Scorsese, then my fiancé, was off in France, and I was being consoled over take-away pizza by his two friends.

Spielberg was talking about a film he longed to make about the UFO phenomenon. There was scant support for the project and Spielberg was discouraged—although the project itself excited him. What to do? De Palma encouraged him to follow his heart and make that piece of art. That movie became *Close Encounters of the Third Kind.*

I tell this story not to drop names, but to make the point that even the most illustrious among our ranks as artists were not always illustrious and won't ever be beyond the fears and doubts that are part of creative territory. These fears and doubts will always, for all of us, be something to move through with a little help from our friends.

We all start out the same way—rich in dreams and nothing more. If we are lucky, we find friends to believe in our dreams with us. When we do, that creative cluster becomes a magnet to attract our good.

I have been teaching *The Artist's Way* for a long time. I've discovered that while I don't believe in a quick fix, rapid and sustained creative gains can be made—especially if people are willing to band together in clusters. When I travel to teach, it is with the goal of leaving creative clusters behind me in each locale so that people can work together to nurture and support each other over the long haul.

In Chicago there is a cluster that has been together for years. The group began with questions like, "Will I be able to write again?" and "I'd like to try to improve, but I'm scared," and "I really want to produce," and, "I'd like to write a play."

Years later, the cluster is the same, but the questions are very different. "Who's throwing Ginny's Emmy nomination party?" and "Should Pam do her third play with the same theater company?"

As creative people, we are meant to encourage one another. That was my goal in writing *The Artist's Way* and it is my goal in teaching it. Your goal, it is my hope, is to encourage each other's dreams as well as your own. Creative ideas are brain*children*. Like all children, they must be birthed and this birthing is both a personal and collective experience.

It was my privilege recently to midwife a book in my own creative cluster. My friend Sonia Choquette, a gifted psychic and teacher, was able to shape her long years of experience into an invaluable tool kit, *The Psychic Pathway*. As her friend, I received her book as nightly instalments on my fax machine. I would fax her back, believing in her when she, like all artists, had trouble believing in herself.

Raised, like so many of us, to hide her creative light under a bushel lest her dazzle diminish the light of others, Sonia experienced doubt, fear and deepening faith as she moved past these creative barriers into creative birth.

I know there are those among you who fear undertaking projects that seem to demand many dark nights of the soul. Let me suggest to you that such nights may also be, in the beautiful Spanish words, *noches estrelladas*—star-studded.

Like neighboring constellations, we can serve each other both as guides and as company. In walking your artist's way, my deepest wish for you is the company of fellow lights and the generosity to light each other's ways as we each pass temporarily into darkness.

Know this well: success occurs in clusters and is born in generosity. Let us form constellations of believing mirrors and move into our powers.

Sacred Circle Rules

1. Creativity flourishes in a place of safety and acceptance.

2. Creativity grows among friends, withers among enemies.

3. All creative ideas are children who deserve our protection.

4. All creative success requires creative failure.

5. Fulfilling our creativity is a sacred trust.

6. Violating someone's creativity violates a sacred trust.

7. Creative feedback must support the creative child, never shame it.

8. Creative feedback must build on strengths, never focus on weaknesses.

Until we accept the fact that life itself is founded in mystery, we shall learn nothing.

HENRY MILLER

I learn by going where I have to go.

THEODORE ROETHKE

9. Success occurs in clusters and is born in generosity.

10. The good of another can never block our own.

Above All: God is the source. No human power can deflect our good or create it. We are all conduits for a higher self that would work through us. We are all equally connected to a spiritual source. We do not always know which among us will teach us best. We are all meant to cherish and serve one another. *The Artist's Way* is tribal. The spirit of service yields us our dharma: that right path we dream of following in our best and most fulfilled moments of faith.

AN ARTIST'S PRAYER

O Great Creator,
We are gathered together in your name
That we may be of greater service to you
And to our fellows.
We offer ourselves to you as instruments.
We open ourselves to your creativity in our lives.
We surrender to you our old ideas.
We welcome your new and more expansive ideas.
We trust that you will lead us.
We know you created us and that creativity
Is your nature and our own.
We ask you to unfold our lives
According to your plan, not our low self-worth.
Help us to believe that it is not too late
And that we are not too small or too flawed
To be healed—
By you and through each other—and made whole.
Help us to love one another,
To nurture each other's unfolding,
To encourage each other's growth,
And understand each other's fears.
Help us to know that we are not alone,
That we are loved and lovable.
Help us to create as an act of worship to you.

READING LIST

My experience as a teacher tells me that those who read this book are better off doing something, rather than reading another book, but I have included many of my favorites just in case they feel compelled to research further. These books represent some of the very best in their fields.

Angeles, Agnes. *The Four-Fold Way*. New York: Harper-Collins, 1993. A big-hearted, lucid guide to creative spiritual practice.

Augros, Robert M., and Stanciu, George N. *The Story of Science*. New York: Bantam Books, 1984.

Bachrach, Arthur. *Psychological Research*. New York: Random House, 1962. A lively book on the creativity in science.

Beattie, Melody, *Beyond Codependency*. Hazleden: Harper, 1987. Excellent for dealing with crazymakers.

———. *Codependent No More*. San Francisco: Harper and Row, 1987. Excellent for breaking the virtue trap.

Becker, Ernest. *The Denial of Death*. New York: Free Press, 1973. Great book about the roots of fear.

Bennett, Hal Zina, and Susan Sparrow. *Follow Your Bliss*. New York: Avon Books, 1990.

Bolen, Jean Shinoda. *The Tao of Psychology*. London: Harper and Row, 1979. An excellent jumping-off point for spiritual seekers.

Bolles, Richard Nelson. *What Color Is Your Parachute?* Berkeley: Ten Speed Press, 1970. Whimsical and pragmatic guide to goal setting.

Bradley, Marion Zimmer. *The Mists of Avalon*. London: Penguin, 1993. A work of fiction which invites and encourages creative spirituality and spiritual creativity.

Bradshaw, John. *Healing the Shame That Binds You*. London: Health Communications, 1988. Superb book for explaining the role of shame in the addiction process.

Brande, Dorothea. *Becoming a Writer*. London: Macmillan, 1983. The best book on writing I've ever found.

Brown, Barbara. *Supermind: The Ultimate Energy*. London: Harper and Row, 1980.

Bryan, Mark, and Cameron, Julia. *The Money Drunk*. New

York: Ballantine Books, 1992. A hands-on toolkit for financial freedom. This book creates new language and a new lens for money management. It grew out of *The Artist's Way* because money is the most often cited block.

Burnham, Sophy. *A Book of Angels*. London: Rider, 1992. An elegant, deeply felt exploration of the spiritual powers and forces at play in our lives.

Butterworth, Eric. *Spiritual Economics: The Prosperity Process*. Unity Village, MO: Unity School of Christianity, 1983. Explains abundance as a spiritual issue.

Came to Believe. New York: Alcoholics Anonymous World Services, 1973. Useful and touching book about embryonic faith.

Edwards, Betty. *Drawing on the Right Side of the Brain*. London: Souvenir Press, 2nd ed. 1992. Seminal book on artist-brain creativity.

Fankhauser, Jerry. *The Power of Affirmations*. Farmingdale, NY: Coleman Graphics, 1983.

Fassel, Diane. *Working Ourselves to Death*. London: Thorsons, rev. ed. 1992.

Ferrucci, Piero. *Inevitable Grace*. Wellingborough: Crucible, 1990.

Fields, Rick; Taylor, Peggy; Weyler, Rex; and Rick Ingrasci. *Chop Wood Carry Water*. Los Angeles: Jeremy P. Tarcher, 1984. Inviting overview of synthesis of East/West spirituality.

Gawain, Shakti. *Creative Visualization*. London: Bantam, 1985. Helpful in learning to create and hold a vision.

_____. *Living in the Light*. London: Eden Grove, 1988. Helpful in understanding recovery as process.

Goldberg, Natalie. *Wild Mind*. London: Rider, 1991. Further notes on the artist's trail.

_____. *Writing Down the Bones*. Boston: Shambala Press, 1986. Distributed through Random House, New York. The wizardly blockbreaker book for writers. Yes, this one really does work.

Grof, Christina, and Stanislav Grof. *The Stormy Search for the Self*. London: Mandala, 1991.

Grof, Christina, and Stanislav Grof, eds. *Spiritual Emergency*. Los Angeles: Jeremy P. Tarcher, 1989.

Harmon, Willis, and Howard Rheingold. *Higher Creativity*. Los Angeles: Jeremy P. Tarcher, 1984.

Hart, Mickey. *Drumming at the Edge of Magic*. San Francisco: HarperCollins, 1990. A great book on music as a spiritual experience.

James, William. *The Varieties of Religious Experience*. London: Harvard University Press, 1985.

Jeffers, Susan. *Feel the Fear and Do It Anyway*. London: Century, 1989. An into-the-water book for getting past fear.

Keyes, Ken. *Handbook for Higher Consciousness*. Coos Bay, OR: Living Love Publications, 1975.

Kornfield, Jack. *A Path With Heart*. New York: Bantam, 1993. A compassionate, invaluable guide for anyone working to appreciate the worth of process as well as product.

Larsen, Earnie. *Stage II Recovery: Life beyond Addiction*. New York: Harper and Row, 1985. How not to be or tolerate a crazymaker.

Leonard, Jim. *Your Fondest Dream*. Cincinnati: Vivation, 1989. An into-the-water book; many brainstorming techniques.

Lewis, C. S. *Miracles*. London: Geoffrey Bles, 1947.

Miller, Alice. *The Drama of Being a Child, and the Search for the True Self*. London: Virago, 1987. Seminal book on how toxic family dynamics dampen creativity.

Nachmanovitch, Stephen. *Free Play*. Los Angeles: Jeremy P. Tarcher, 1991. A wonderful book on creative freedom.

Norwood, Robin. *Letters from Women Who Love Too Much*. London: Arrow, 1988. Seminal work on codependency.

Orsborn, Carol. *Enough Is Enough: Exploding the Myth of Having It All*. New York: G. P. Putnam's Sons, 1986. Excellent for helping dismantle the heroic workaholic personality.

Ostrander, Sheila, and Lynn Schroeder. *Superlearning*. London: Souvenir Press, 1979.

Pagels, Elaine. *The Gnostic Gospels*. London: Penguin, 1982.

Peck, M. Scott. *The Road Less Travelled*. London: Arrow, 1990. A book for early spiritual skeptics.

Rich, Adrienne, ed. *On Lies, Secrets, and Silence: Selected Prose*. London: Virago, 1980. Title essay brilliantly explores the effect of secrets and shame on personal relationships.

Roethke, Theodore. *Collected Poems*. London: Anchor Press, 1975. Poet as mystic.

Roman, Sanaya, and Duane Packer. *Creating Money*. Tiburon, CA: H. J. Kramer, 1988.

Russ, Joanna. *How to Suppress Women's Writing*. London: Women's Press, 1984. Hilarious and brilliant book on why we get blocked.

Schaef, Anne Wilson. *Escape from Intimacy*. London: Thorsons, 1992.

————. *Meditations for Women Who Do Too Much*. San Francisco: Harper, 1990.

Sex and Love Addicts Anonymous. Boston: The Augustine Fellowship. Sex and Love Addicts Anonymous Fellowship-Wide Services, 1986. One of the best books on addiction. The chapters on withdrawal and building partnerships should be required reading.

Shaughnessy, Susan. *Walking on Alligators*. New York: HarperCollins, 1993. A companionable savvy guide for anyone working to appreciate the worth of process as well as product.

Starhawk. *The Spiral Dance*. London: Harper and Row, 1979. Brilliant on creativity and god/goddess within.

Wegscheider-Cruse, Sharon. *Choicemaking: For Co-dependents, Adult Children and Spirituality Seekers*. Pompano Beach, FL: Health Communications, 1985. Recommended for dismantling codependent workaholism.

Whitfield, Charles. *Healing the Child Within*. Deerfield Beach, FL: Health Communications, 1987.

Winn, Marie. *The Plug-in Drug: Television, Children, and the Family*. London: Penguin, rev. ed. 1985.

Woititz, Janet. *Home Away from Home: The Art of Self-Sabotage*. Pompano Beach, FL: Health Communications, 1987. Important for arresting the mechanism of aborting success.

————. *Struggle for Intimacy*. Pompano Beach, FL: Health Communications, 1985.

INDEX

ACKNOWLEDGEMENTS

I WISH TO ACKNOWLEDGE my creative colleague, Edmund Towle, who faithfully road-tested these principles, and whose feedback I found invaluable. I wish to thank Julianna McCarthy, Gerald Ayres, John Nichols and Sir Anthony Hopkins for their personal creative courage and their generosity in the encouragement of others' creativity. I salute Timothy Wheater for creating a body of sound that encourages and creates a body of light. His healing music has proved invaluable to this work. I thank my agent Susan Schulman for her astringent wit and perspicacity. Additionally, the Reverends Sara and Mike Matoin of Unity, Chicago; Michele Lowrance, Laura Leddy Waldron, Ginny Weissman, Michelle Citron, Kathy Churay, and Marilyn Lieberman; Howard Mandel and Gayle Seminara of Transitions Bookstore, Chicago. Most especially I wish to acknowledge my students and the inspired editorial guidance of Jan Johnson, Rick Benzel, and Jeremy Tarcher, publisher and rainmaker. It's my belief that the Great Creator led us all.

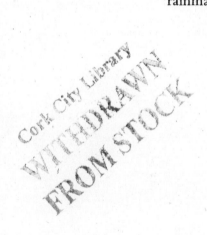